DO MEMBERS OF CONGRESS REWARD THEIR FUTURE EMPLOYERS?

Evaluating the Revolving Door Syndrome

Adolfo Santos

University Press of America,® Inc.
Lanham · Boulder · New York · Toronto · Oxford

Copyright © 2006 by
University Press of America,® Inc.
4501 Forbes Boulevard
Suite 200
Lanham, Maryland 20706
UPA Acquisitions Department (301) 459-3366

PO Box 317
Oxford
OX2 9RU, UK

Library of Congress Control Number: 2005932735
ISBN 0-7618-3329-3 (paperback : alk. ppr.)

To Betin

whose affection sustains me

Content

Preface

The vast majority of public servants have a genuine devotion to their country, its institutions, and their fellow citizens. Many public servants could easily earn higher incomes in the private sector. Many could easily find positions that are more satisfying, prestigious and convenient than those of public servants. Regardless of their ideological position, most public servants serve with the intent of making their cities, their state and their country a better place for themselves and for posterity. This, I believe to be true. In the pages to follow I will focus on public servants who leave the public sector to become lobbyists. I will focus on a particularly powerful public servant – the former member of Congress. I will argue that in their becoming lobbyists, former members of Congress could potentially jeopardize the very public policy that they are entrusted to create. I will argue that former members of Congress, in their capacity to plan their exit from Congress, are in a position to exploit their ability to create policy that could benefit the very groups that may want to employ them later.

I have gathered data on hundreds of former members of Congress who served between the early 1970s and the early 2000s. Great care was taken to identify former members of Congress and their post-congressional employment experience. This book relies on both statistical data that was gathered over the course of several years, and anecdotal evidence that has been reported by the popular press. The evidence suggests that former members of Congress who become lobbyists behave differently than their counterparts who do not become lobbyists during their last term in office. The legislative activity of lawmakers who are serving their last term in office can be explained, in part, by their post-congressional lobbying activity. What lawmakers do during their last term in office is a function of what they do when they leave office.

Several cases will be presented to indicate the danger associated with post-congressional lobbying. The cases will provide examples of lawmakers who successfully protected special interests only to be employed by these special interests upon leaving office. The practice of lobbying after leaving office is one that is growing. It is also a practice that does not seem to be stymied by temporary bans on post-congressional lobbying. What was once viewed as inappropriate behavior has become so acceptable that some of the most prominent public figures in the US government today have registered as lobbyists.

Introduction

In 1957, the *Congressional Quarterly Almanac* reported that less than a dozen former members of Congress were registered as lobbyists (1957,739). By 1994, Congressional Quarterly reported that 25 percent of former members of Congress found their way back into the Capitol representing special interests (Eilperin 1996). In 1999, the Center for Responsive Politics listed 138 former members of Congress as registered lobbyists[1]. The dramatic increase in the number of former members of Congress who are finding themselves serving as lobbyists, raises concerns about the extent to which the public interest is undermined by the post-congressional ambitions of members of Congress. Former members of Congress are finding themselves in positions to profit from their congressional careers in ways that are not constrained by the electorate and that may place public policy in jeopardy (Carr 1996, 1517). This *revolving door* syndrome, which allows high-ranking public officials to leave public life only to see themselves return as lobbyists after a brief hiatus, threatens the very legitimacy of those political institutions that these individuals once served. The fear is that members of Congress may use their public posts for private gain, either by rewarding, or at least by sponsoring legislation that sends signals to prospective employers. It is the purpose of this book to evaluate the extent to which former members of Congress become lobbyists, and the implications of this career choice on pubic policy.

This question is addressed using a variety of empirical data, addressing separate components of the overall question. First, I begin by asking whether there has been a change in the post-congressional behavior of members of

Congress. This becomes important because the claim will be made that the post-congressional behavior of members of Congress has been driven by the changes that occurred in Congress during the early 1970s. During this period a variety of changes occurred to the political environment. The peculiar combination of congressional and campaign reforms in conjunction with the rising complexity of public policy led to a political climate that brought interest groups in closer contact with legislators. And, as legislators reformed the campaign system, they would become increasingly beholden to political action committees and special interests that could assist them in their electoral campaigns. This closer contact with lobbyists and interest groups has improved the likelihood that former members of Congress will move from the floor to the lobby[2].

Of concern is whether or not members of Congress with post-congressional lobbying ambitions are using their positions to maximize the interests of those they plan to serve once they leave office. In addressing this question we begin by asking, is there a difference between those who lobby and those who do not in terms of their legislative activity just before they leave office? Is there a connection between the groups that they go to work for and the areas of specialization that they developed while serving in Congress? And finally, is there a connection between the bills that members of Congress sponsor and the groups that will employ them? And perhaps more importantly, do these bills become laws? In addressing these questions we are able to evaluate the nature and extent to which former members of Congress abuse their positions as public servants.

Two Models Of Behavior

The literature which, evaluates the behavior of members of Congress during their last term, can be broadly categories into two groups. One perspective indicates that members of Congress become *lame ducks* during their last term (Prewitt 1969, Frantzich 1978, Hook 1992, Herrick, Moore and Hibbing 1994). Members of Congress who are serving out their last term become legislatively inactive (Frantzich 1978). They also become less inclined to keep in touch with their constituents (Herrick, Moore and Hibbing 1994,224). In a sense, members serving out their last term tend to slack off as representatives. But, just as they compromise the representation of their constituents, they also compromise their reputations. And by compromising their reputations, they also compromise their employment opportunities upon leaving office (see Lott 1990). But not all members of Congress who are serving out their last term are lame duck representatives. Some observers have found evidence that members of Congress actually improve as representatives when they are serving out their last term (Lott and Reed 1989, Lott 1990, Jacobson 1992, Lott and Davis 1992, Herrick, Moore and Hibbing 1994). This second perspective takes two competing positions. Either members of Congress are liberated from the constraints of the electorate (Herrick, Moore and Hibbing 1994) or, the members have been improving over time, and so, as they approach the end of their service, they are most in tune with their constituents (Lott and Reed 1989). It will be argued that what these observers perceive to be improvements are manifestations of retiring members of Congress preparing their exit.

Structure Of The Book

The layout of the book is simple. It begins by laying out the theoretical importance of the thesis. It then quickly covers the context in which post-congressional lobbying has evolved. The causes and consequences of post-congressional career patterns are developed in chapters three, four and five. The text concludes with an analysis of the findings in a broader context, and then suggests alternatives to confronting the threat to public policy in ways that do not undermine individual liberty or the legislative process. Chapter one addresses the theoretical implications of post-congressional lobbying. The chapter begins by addressing the concept of representation. This in turn raises questions regarding the extent to which the Madisonian model, which relies heavily on institutional factors to maximize political representation, is able to curtail the ambitions of individual members of Congress. The conclusion drawn from this analysis is that the Madisonian model works best under the assumption that members of Congress seek only to remain in public life. This is an assumption that, as we shall see, is not only unrealistic but also damaging to American political representation.

Chapter two discusses the contextual framework in which post-congressional behavior has advanced. The context is discussed addressing three questions. First, what changes have occurred in Congress that may have impacted the behavior of members of Congress? Second, how have members of Congress changed to allow for the behavior that we are witnessing today? And Finally, how has Washington DC changed over the years and to what extent has the change made it more agreeable to former members of Congress as a place to live? These three questions help paint a picture of the political, social and environmental context in which the behavior of members of Congress has evolved.

Chapter three addresses the question of who becomes a lobbyist. The focus here is on individual and institutional characteristics. The conclusion that can be drawn is that those with greater experience and political power become valuable to lobbying firms and special interests. This is underscored by the fact that a sizeable number of high-ranking members of the more powerful committees have had a greater frequency of becoming lobbyists.

Chapters four through six draw a clearer connection between public policy and post-congressional lobbying. Chapter four takes the first step by asking whether there is a difference in the legislative activity of two sets of retiring former members of Congress. One group consists of those who would become lobbyists upon leaving office, and the other consists of those who would not become lobbyists upon leaving office. In this chapter, findings are presented which indicate that there are real differences between the two groups, with post-congressional lobbyists remaining considerably more active during their last term than those who do not become lobbyists. The evidence suggests that members are either using their positions to send signals to prospective employers, or they are rewarding their future employers with favorable legislation. In chapter five, we develop the possibility that the former members of Congress are using their positions as a steppingstone for some future employment. A connection is drawn between the post-congressional careers of former members of Congress and their legislative work while in office. Several case studies are presented, indicating that members of Congress may be doing more than simply sending signals to indicate their policy expertise to special interests. Former members of Congress do sponsor bills that will have a direct and positive bearing on the industries and groups that the lawmakers will go to lobby for upon leaving office[3].

Chapter six further elaborates on the implications of post-congressional lobbying. The chapter presents instances in which post-congressional lobbying careers have brought former members of Congress in direct opposition to US Foreign policy. Post-congressional lobbyists, serving as foreign agents, have lobbied on behalf of countries with policy positions antithetical to US policy. The chapter also discusses the impact that post-congressional lobbying can have on the legitimacy of American political institutions, i.e. Congress.

Chapter seven concludes by further elaborating on the problems posed by post-congressional lobbying to the credibility of the political institution. And we revisit James Madison and his attempt to maximize both political representation and liberty. A set of solutions is presented which not only maintains the liberty of individual members of Congress, but also improves the quality of representation without compromising public policy. As Congress has changed in modern times, we begin to see that a new type of public servant has arisen, one that is less inclined to see public service and representation as an end. This new representative sees representation as a means to an end. And this is of fundamental concern, because, as has been witnessed in modern times, American political institutions have suffered a serious decline in the level of support granted to them by the American people. If the legislative branch continues to suffer such declines, its legitimacy and credibility may be undermined in ways that may make it impossible for Congress to recover.

---

[1] See www.opensecrets.org/pubs/lobby98/formerreps.htm.

---

[2] It should be noted that former members of Congress are given special privileges to walk on the floor of either the House or the Senate.

[3] See the case of Toby Roth in Chapter 1.

1

James Madison And The Revolving Door

Before retiring from the 104th Congress, Toby Roth was the fourth ranking Republican on the International Relations Committee and Chair of the Subcommittee on International Economic Policy and Trade. In this capacity, Toby Roth, in conjunction with National Security Adviser Anthony Lake, fashioned a trade agreement that allowed Hughes Electronics Corporation to export satellites and other sensitive equipment to China. Two years after leaving office, Toby Roth is working for Hughes Electronics, among others, as a lobbyist. In 1998, Congress and the White House began to raise serious questions about the extent to which the trade deal that improved Hughes Electronics' three billion dollar market with China might have compromised national security (Mintz 1998). And, while it was common knowledge that Toby Roth would not be seeking reelection, he remained active during his last term, ensuring that those groups that would later employ him as a lobbyist received support from him while he was still in office.

Toby Roth's case raises questions about the extent to which members of Congress who have their own discrete ambitions compromise the public interest. The issue is one of representation, and the extent to which public officials can be constrained by the electoral process to do what is in the interest of the constituency without undermining the integrity of public policy. But this in itself raises other concerns. At the core of the problem is a conflict between two critical components of legislative institutions – representation and political ambition. Legislative institutions, if they are to function democratically, must represent the wishes of the public. But, in order for the public to have its wishes represented adequately, ambitious individuals must desire to serve as representatives. The concern, of course, was at the time of the nation's founding and continues to be, keeping ambition in check. The framers of the Constitution believed that they had developed a solution to the problem of constraining ambition while maximizing representation through the use of frequent elections.

American democracy would in essence rely heavily on ambitious individuals, but it is these very ambitious individuals who may undermine the representative process.

The purpose of this chapter is to explain the theoretical and practical importance of understanding the post-congressional career goals of members of Congress, and the implications of those career choices on public policy. I begin with a brief discussion on the concept of political representation. While by no means an exhaustive evaluation of the literature on political representation, this section presents a key distinction between the Burkean model of representation and the Madisonian model. While the former relies heavily on a natural aristocracy to insure that the public good is protected in a legislative body, the latter relies almost exclusively on the structure of political institutions to accomplish the same goal. The Madisonian model, however well thought out it may be, reaches a point in which the structure of the legislative branch, and its reliance on voters and ambitious candidates, fails to constrain the behavior of members of Congress.

Ambition is what we hope to understand. This is the driving force of public officials. Whether they seek a higher office, to remain in their existing chamber, or to leave public life; the ambitions of public officials can be understood by their behavior. And, while there are many components to their behavior, we seek to understand their legislative behavior. What type of public policy do they sponsor? In which committees do they serve? And, who benefits from the legislation? In the sections that follow the discussion on representation, I develop the concept of political ambition within the confines of the research topic. Essentially, I argue that one of the most understudied forms of political ambition – discrete ambition – is one of the most damaging to the representative process and the legitimacy of political institutions. I argue that discrete ambition is threatening the legitimacy of the US Congress, and the representative process in general, because many members are using Congress as a steppingstone to a lobbying career. And, if these members are using their positions as representatives to reward groups whom they are to be employed by upon leaving Congress, then the public good may very well be compromised. The two sections that follow the discussion on political ambition focus on the development of the lobbying industry and the recent developments in legislative activity and public policy.

The growth of the lobbying industry can be explained by several factors. On the one hand, the growth has been fueled by the phenomenal legislative activity of the New Deal and the Great Society programs. This is a view echoed by Kilian and Sawislak who point out that the increased production of public policy has spawned the dependents of public policy – interest groups, lobbyists, law firms, and think tanks (1982,201). The volume and more recently, the complexity of public policy has spawned a lobbying industry, which in turn, has led to an increased demand for policy experts to plead their cases before governmental institutions. And, as it happens, former members of Congress fit this description. While legislative activity and its complexity have fueled the growth of the lobbying industry, members of Congress have been forced to come into greater contact with special interests. Members of Congress rely on special interests for information on legislation, funding legislative campaigns, and to rally support (Schlozman and Tierney 1986, Heinz, Laumann, Nelson and Salisbury 1993). Members of Congress rely on special interest groups for policy expertise, and by some accounts, on the actual drafting of bills (Schlozman and Tierney 1986 and Heinz et al. 1993). Further bringing lawmakers and lobbyists into close contact have been changes in the way candidates fund political campaigns. The Watergate scandal brought with it campaign reforms, which outlawed large campaign contributions. The outlawing of large campaign contributions heightened the role of the lobbyist. Lobbyists were in a position to bring in large numbers of legal contributions from the groups and individuals that they represented. It is this close contact and interdependence between members of Congress and lobbyists that create the appearance of *quid pro quo*, in which something is expected in return for a service. Whether it is campaign contributions, support from colleagues, or promises of future employment, this atmosphere threatens the legitimacy of the political institution and the public interest.

Congress And Representation

The eighteenth century British statesman and political thinker Edmund Burke, writing in the late 1700s, defined the concept of representation as being a trusteeship between the represented and the representative. He took the position that a natural aristocracy existed for the purpose of governance (Burke 1791[1962]). The aristocracy represented and protected the interest of the commonwealth by discovering and enacting the common good (Pitkin 1967, 169). While a modern representative might be more inclined to look to the representative's constituents for guidance on what action to take, the natural aristocracy, through reason, could identify the public good. From Edmund Burke's perspective, the interest of the commonwealth could be determined through the power of reason, rather than by surveying the populace for their interest. The representative must deduce the nation's interest. This requires that the representative put aside the interests of constituencies, and instead contemplate the interests of the nation as a whole. "This is the center of our unity", wrote Edmund Burke, "This government of reference is a trustee for the whole, and not for the parts" (1790 [1950], 207-208). It is a government that circumvents the concerns of individual interests, for the sake of the nation as a whole. Those chosen to represent are not to represent the concerns of individual districts, or the voters. They are to represent the wishes of the commonwealth. Edmund Burke writes:

> The King is the representative of the people; so are the lords; so are the judges. They all are trustees for the people, as well as the commons; because no power is given for the sole sake of the holder; and although government certainly is an institution of divine authority, yet its forms, and the persons who administer it, all originate from the people (Burke 1770 [1999], 118).

This conceptualization of representation contributed to the tension between the American colonies and the British crown. While the American colonists insisted that they were not receiving adequate representation in the House of Commons, the King's response was that every British representative represented the interests of the colonists given that the colonies were British domain. King George's understanding of representation was that the individual members of parliament were serving as trustees.

The quality of the representatives is one of the major features of the Burkean model of representation. Edmund Burke would write, "There is no qualification for government but virtue and wisdom" (1790). The natural aristocracy is the one group that is in a position to make choices about what is right and wrong. But this does not mean that the aristocracy is one of intellectuals, rather, it is one of virtuous individuals (1790). This group possesses both a moral and intellectual capacity that allows it to make practical decisions about others. But in order for the natural aristocracy to function properly, it must be able to separate itself from the public. The governing body must remain clear of those who do not belong to the natural aristocracy. If the governing body is not restricted to the natural aristocracy, he argues, it will make the few possessors of virtue the tools of those with "sinister ambition and a lust of meretricious glory" (1790). For Burke, ambition is an evil that can be circumvented by virtuous individuals alone.

Across the Atlantic, different understanding of representation was developing. The most cogent articulation of this new conceptualization of representation comes from James Madison. The American model of representation as presented by James Madison minimizes the importance of virtue and exploits political ambition. While Edmund Burke's conceptualization of representation depends on the ethical and moral character of elected officials, James Madison relies heavily on the structure of political institutions as instruments that insure the public good. The Madisonian model focuses almost exclusively on the establishment of political institutions that will ensure representation in spite of who is elected into office. Madison does not rely on the natural aristocracy to govern. "Enlightened statesmen will not always be at the helm", writes Madison in Federalist Ten (1787). It was believed, by Madison and others, that the organization of a political institution could ensure that the government represented the public good, absent the presence of enlightened statesmen. The framers of the Constitution were keenly aware that in order for the political system to work, it could not depend on virtuous individuals disinterested in preserving or improving their personal lot. The political system that was created by the framers of the Constitution assumed human nature to be driven by ambition, and harnessing this ambition would insure representation without undermining liberty. The framers, thus, were attempting to control human nature by binding it to the institutional structure (Hamilton, Madison and Jay, Federalist 10 and 51 [1788] 1990, 267). The chief method of binding the individual's ambition would be through the use of elections (Hamilton, Madison and Jay, Federalist 57 [1788] 1990, 296). Publius writes:

> As it is essential to liberty that the government in general, should have a common interest with the people; so it is particularly essential that the branch of it under consideration, should have as immediate dependence on, and an intimate sympathy with the people. Frequent elections are unquestionably the only policy by which this dependence and sympathy can be effectually secured (Madison, Hamilton and Jay, Federalist 52 [1788] 1990, 274).

Representatives interested in holding on to power would be compelled to represent the interest of the people. Ambition would be "made to counteract ambition" (Madison, Hamilton and Jay, Federalist 51 [1788] 1990, 267). Failure to represent the interest of the constituency would lead competitors to challenge the incumbent official, leading the electorate to vote those incumbents who were not representing adequately out of office. The result has been that the Constitution has created political institutions that simplify human motives, making the behavior of elected officials "understandable and predictable" (Schlesinger 1966, 2).

The framers of the Constitution set out to create a republic in which individuals would represent the interests of their constituents. Representation would occur because those elected to public office would desire to hold those seats, and in order to hold on to those seats they would serve the interests of their constituents. Elections, however, serve a meaningful role in controlling the ambitions of representatives only to the degree that elected official want to remain in office. James Madison cautions that representatives "will be compelled to anticipate the moment when their power is to cease" (Federalist 57 [1788] 1990, 290). If representatives hold ambitions that extend beyond their public lives, then those discrete ambitions may influence how the representatives behave in their public life. The electoral system will only serve to control the ambitions of those who desire to stay in office. Once the public official no longer cares to remain in office, elections no longer constrain the ambitions of individuals.

Ambition

The ambition that Madison hoped to regulate could only be kept in check under specific circumstances. These specific circumstances would require that the public official want to remain in office or seek a higher office. Those planning to remain in public life, either in their existing position or in some higher office, would be expected to serve the public interest so as not to compromise their standing. It is likely that many public officials may harbor personal ambitions that are not so easily controlled by the electoral system. While it is quite likely that not all ambitions are controlled by frequent elections, American democracy depends in good part on the ability of the system to undermine the personal ambitions of public officials if the ambitions are not consistent with the public interest. It should be noted, however, that ambition is generally not viewed as a danger, but as an instrument of good government. Without a steady supply of ambitious individuals, democracy in America is not possible. Ambitious individuals will run for office and will be driven to continue to serve. Because of their desire to win re-election, they will be compelled to represent their constituents' interests and it is their constituents who will control their ambitions. An understanding of ambition, therefore, adds to the theory of representation by presenting the idea that the future ambitions of representatives shape their behavior while in office (Prewitt and Nowlin 1969, 299). Ambition's function in the democratic process, therefore, is an important one, and one that requires a clearer understanding.

Perhaps the best attempt to understand the concept of political ambition is presented by Joseph Schlesinger. He identifies three types of congressional ambitions – *progressive, static* and *discrete ambitions*. The first of these, progressive ambition - refers to the politician's desire to move up to more powerful offices, while static ambition refers to a public official's desire to make a career out of a particular office. Discrete ambition, by contrast, refers to the desire to serve for a limited time period and then withdrawing from public life (Schlesinger 1966, 10). It is the last of these that I believe presents the most serious challenge to the Madisonian model. In the following section, I will elaborate on the three concepts of ambition.

Progressive Ambition

Work on ambition theory in the political science literature has generally focused on "progressive ambition" at the expense of static or discrete ambition (Abramson, Aldrich and Rohde, 1987; Brace 1984; Prewitt and Nowlin 1969; Rohde 1979; Schlesinger 1966). Much of this work attempts to describe and explain the behavior of members of legislative bodies who have goals for higher offices. Paul Hain for instance has found a relationship between the progressive goals of state legislators and their age (1974). Rohde, also attempting to explain progressive ambition, has found that those hoping to advance to a higher office evaluate their chances of winning, as well as determine the costs and benefits of attempting to advance to a higher office (1979). Others have found clear evidence that the behavior of those members of Congress who plan to seek a higher office tend to have broader policy goals than those who do not (Prewitt and Nowlin 1969). And, their roll-call votes tend to change depending on whether they are seeking a higher office or not (Hibbing 1986).

Static Ambition

Members of Congress who have static ambitions arrive to their seats with the intention of holding on to them for as long as they can. While this type of ambition has been relatively ignored, it manifests itself in the declining turnover rates that Congress has experienced in modern times. Although rarely mentioned, static ambition has been taken for granted by political scientists like Anthony Downs (1957) and David Mayhew (1974) when they argue that elected officials have one central goal - winning reelection. And many members, at least during much of this century, have had good reason to remain in their seats. The seniority rule rewarded those who could hold on to their seats the longest with committee chair positions. With time, congressional service has become more prestigious and formal, leading to longer tenures (Polsby 1968). The proactive nature of government during the periods of the New Deal and the Great Society also encouraged representatives to stay in office longer. But congressional change, brought on during the late 1960s and early 1970s, led to a sudden increase in the number of members of Congress who were voluntarily retiring from office (Hibbing 1982b). Some claiming that serving in Congress was simply "no fun" anymore, with members increasingly becoming disaffected with service (Cooper and West 1981, Theriault 1998).

Discrete Ambition

Moore and Hibbing have questioned the extent to which credence can be given to the argument that members of Congress were leaving voluntarily because serving was no longer fun (1998). They argue that there are other contextual factors that drive the choice to leave office. Members of Congress have left office voluntarily because they have ulterior motives. Hall and Van Houweling, for instance, have found that recent increases in voluntary retirement have been due to members' desires to capitalize on lucrative pensions (1995). John Hibbing, similarly, finds that pension improvements affect the rate of voluntary retirement (1982b). Others have found that members left voluntarily in 1992 because this would be the last time that members would be allowed to keep unspent campaign contributions (Groseclose and Krehbiel 1994, Borders and Dockery 1995). These examples serve as evidence that personal avarice and ambition play a role in the calculus to leave office. It would not be too far removed that other post-congressional ambitions might also prompt members to retire. Once members of Congress no longer desire to be members of Congress, then the capacity of the electoral system to compel the representatives to *represent* falls apart. Once members of Congress no longer seek reelection, creating public policy, or gaining influence in Congress as goals, then the members of Congress are no longer constrained by the demands of their constituents. The use of elections to constrain ambition is a useful tool, but it is only useful at constraining progressive and static ambition.

Once the ambitions of members of Congress change from being progressive or static to discrete, then political representation comes under the very serious threat of being undermined. The potential problem posed by discrete ambition has, unfortunately, been virtually ignored in the political science literature. Rohde, for instance, has written:

> We say "almost all" (members of the House hold progressive ambition) because we believe that discrete ambition should be maintained as a separate category. There are some members of the House who begin service with the intent of simply filling out the present term. The most obvious case of this is the wife of a deceased member who agrees to run in a special election to fill the vacancy and serve only as a "care taker" until the next regular election. Such cases are, we believe, few and uninteresting (1979, 3).

The dismissal of cases of discrete ambition as being "few and uninteresting" is a serious mistake. Increasingly, these cases are neither few nor uninteresting. It is important that to note that discrete ambition is held by many more representatives than just those rare cases where widows fill a seat on a temporary basis. The error occurs because of our misunderstanding of the term. The thrust of discrete ambition is not a short tenure, or simply seeing ones term end. The thrust of discrete ambition refers to the goals and desires that a member of Congress has upon retiring from public life.

For some members of Congress, their discrete ambitions may simply be to retire to a sunnier climate, or to spend time with family and friends. But for others, their discrete ambitions may be to profit from their congressional career. Members of Congress may have the desire to become lobbyists or consultants upon the completion of their congressional career. Elected officials who are on the verge of leaving elected office may have post-congressional ambitions that conflict with their representative role while they remain in office. And, if their behavior changes to compensate for those ambitions, they may create public policy that runs counter to the interests of the representative's constituency. This possibility draws attention to the importance of understanding discrete ambition and the role of congressional retirement patterns. Where a member of Congress chooses to retire, and what function he or she chooses to perform upon leaving office, serve as manifestations of discrete ambition. Members of Congress who stay in Washington DC and become lobbyists often times have been driven by discrete ambitions during their last term of office. This leads these members of Congress to sponsor policy that will benefit their future employers.

Interest Group Politics

Since the nation's founding there has been an explicit understanding that interest groups (or what Madison called factions) are a natural part of democratic systems (see Federalist 10, 1787). The framers of the Constitution were concerned, however, with the deleterious effects of factions. Madison wrote:

> By a faction, I understand a number of citizens, whether amounting to a majority or a minority of the whole, who are united and actuated by some common impulse of passion, or interest, adverse to the rights of other citizens, or to the permanent and aggregate interest of the community (Federalist 10 1787).

But rather than constrain factions, Madison felt it more prudent to use the natural inclinations of individuals, and encourage the formation of factions to create a representative government. The desire has been to create a representative government that would protect the rights of individuals and minorities.

The framers of the Constitution would attempt to protect the rights of individuals and minority populations in two ways. First, the framers immediately amended the Constitution with the Bill of Rights, which guarantees everyone certain liberties. For the purposes of this discussion one must turn to the First Amendment, and specifically the right to petition the government. The right to petition the government permits lobbying groups and individuals to solicit the government. This freedom has encouraged the formation of interest groups, insuring that groups will be guaranteed the right to lobby the government. The second method of protecting the rights of individuals is achieved through the segmentation of society. Madison believed that by dividing the population around narrow interests it would be difficult for majorities to form[1]. Madison believed that the nation's huge size and structure of government would create just such a plural society (Federalist 10, 1787). The extended republic would encompass a diversity of interests, which the federal system, in conjunction with the separation of powers, would provide a variety of avenues in which different interests could voice their concerns. Not only could a particular interest appeal to public officials at the local, state and nation levels; but it could also plead its case before the legislative, executive and judicial branches of government. This variety of governmental entities would allow groups to appeal their cases at many different levels – rewarding the groups in some instances and not so in others. The very structure of the new republic would encourage the formation of factions.

Even though Alexis DeTocqueville had observed the American people's penchant for forming associations early in the nineteenth century, the proliferation of interest groups in American Politics did not occur until well into this century. As late as 1920, U.S. Steel was the only corporation with lobbying offices in Washington DC, and by 1940 the number of major corporations with permanent office in Washington had risen to a mere five (Shaiko 1998). Most interest groups formed after World War II, with a large number of these organizing after the 1960s (Walker 1983). By 1968, 34 percent of large corporations had offices in Washington DC (Epstein 1969, 90). And this growth is not totally driven by business interests. A large number of special interests have evolved around causes, or a single issue – a sizable number of these forming after 1975 (Walker 1983). Many special interest groups have found it useful to locate their headquarters in Washington DC or the surrounding area (Colgate 1984). The growth of well organized groups, and their subsequent representation in Washington DC has meant that the Madisonian view of a pluralistic society has evolved as the framers intended, and second that the US Congress is where these groups clash. The concentration of these groups in Washington brings public officials closer together with lobbyists and special interests in ways that promote the creation of public policy while at the same time forming cozy relationships among the actors.

The growth of organized interests has meant greater "conflict between competing coalitions" (Berry 1989, 239). The growth, in conjunction with the increased competitiveness of the industry has led supporters of the pluralist theory to conclude that American politics is functioning, as it should. Critics, however, counter that the growth of the industry serves as an indicator of instability. According to David Truman, interest groups form "in waves", organizing to create a balance in an otherwise unbalanced environment (1971, 59). A different criticism levied against interest group politics is that groups essentially get what they want. Ted Lowi argues that "interest-group liberalism" "provides the system with stability by spreading a sense of representation" (1979, 62). But it is the government that is promoting the growth of the lobbying industry by rewarding special interests with much of what interest groups want. The question remains – to what extent do representatives benefit from the growth of special interest? Whether public officials encourage the growth by rewarding as many special interest groups as possible, or by creating instability in the system, the chief beneficiaries of this environment are the public officials themselves. Not only do a greater number of interest groups lead to an increase in the quantity and quality of information that is available to representatives, interest groups also increase the sources of monetary contributions to fund campaigns.

When Abraham Lincoln ran for office in 1846 he claims to have spent relatively little money on his campaign. Lincoln wrote:

> I made the canvass on my own horse; my entertainment, being at the houses of friends, cost me nothing; and my only outlays was 75 cents for a barrel of cider, which some farm-hands insisted I should treat them to (Sandburg 1926,344).

The cost of running campaigns has increased substantially since then. In 1978, candidates running for congressional office would spend 194.8 million dollars (Federal Election Commission 1995). By 2004 congressional campaigns would spend 911.8 million dollars (Federal Election Commission 2005). The Federal Election Campaign Act of 1971, its subsequent amendments and the Supreme Court decision *Buckley v. Valeo* have greatly changed the interaction between members of Congress and interest groups. The changes in the law now regulate the amount of money that individuals and most organizations can contribute to individual candidates. However, the restrictions on political action committees are much less restrictive, allowing PACs to spend unlimited amounts of money. This has made PACs extremely important actors in political campaigns. And their importance is highlighted by their growth. In 1974 there were a mere 89 corporate PACs. By the 1997-1998 election cycle that figure had ballooned to 1,646 (Federal Election Commission 1999). With the rising cost of political campaigns, special interests and political action committees have become useful allies for politicians.

The increased reliance on special interests for campaign financing, and the increasingly active federal government, bring lobbyists and members of Congress in closer contact with one another. The interaction between members of Congress and interest groups has led to a mutual relationship between the two groups, which extends beyond a professional relationship. Until recently, it was not uncommon for members of Congress to take trips with lobbyists, or to be treated to dinner. Some researchers have found that direct personal contact is the most effective methods in which lobbyists influence members of Congress (Milbrath 1963 and Berry 1977, see also Baumgartner and Leech 1998, 151). Interest groups have gone so far as to draft legislation and regulations (Schlozman and Tierney 1986 and Heinz et. al. 1993). These activities bring members of Congress in relatively close contact with lobbyists and special interest, allowing for personal relationships to develop, which go beyond that of an interest group pressuring a public official. And these relationships manifest themselves well after the member of Congress has left office. There have been changes in American politics in recent years, which suggest that the relationship is much more complex than previously perceived. The cozy triangle in which members of Congress, lobbyists, and administration officials formed close working relationships has been replaced by more complex relationships[2]. These more complex relationships reflect more complex public policy.

Public Policy And The Need For Policy Expertise

The complexity of public policy can be attributed to a variety of sources. First, society has become more complex. While the framers may have had the intention of creating a relatively inactive government, the demands placed upon governments have increased greatly in modern times. Add to this greater demand, changes within governmental institutions that have contributed to the specialization of functions and knowledge for individuals within those institutions, and the end result is a considerably active government producing considerably more complex public policy.

Even if the electoral system is not sufficient to constrain the ambitions of members of Congress, the structure of the institution makes it relatively difficult for policy to be enacted, thus keeping a check on policy. Hanna Pitkin indicates that Madison attempts to maintain stability, not simply by keeping a check on elected officials through the electoral process, but by creating stalemates in government (1967,195). The function of a representative government is to bring groups that are in conflict together. Conflicting groups bring their petitions before the legislative body with the intent of solving their disputes. But the bringing together of competing groups serves not simply to take the dispute out of the social arena and bringing it into the political arena. It serves the purpose of allowing tempers to cool. It is in the legislature, with the passage of time, that cooler heads will prevail (Pitkin 1967, 195-196). A representative government will function best by taking slow and deliberate steps in creating public policy. The function of Madison's representative government will therefore be to maintain the status quo, argues Pitkin (1967,196).

But history suggests that this has not always been the case, particularly during two critical periods of the 20th century – during Franklin Roosevelt's "New Deal" policies, and again during Lyndon Johnson's "Great Society" programs. During these two periods the United States witnessed a period of great change. The federal government during these times sponsored numerous pieces of major legislation, changing the dynamics of inactivity that Pitkin finds in Madison. These two periods in American politics have opened the door for increased legislative activity and increased policy complexity. Representative Joseph W. Martin of Massachusetts remembers when he first entered Congress in the 1920s:

> From one end of a session to another Congress would scarcely have
> three or four issues of consequence besides appropriations bills. And

> the issues themselves were fundamentally simpler than those that
> surge in upon us today in such a torrent that the individual member
> cannot analyze all of them adequately before he is compelled to vote
> (Martin and Donovan 1960, 49-50).

By much of the 20th century, members of Congress would spend nine months out
of every twenty-four in session. More recently, Congress has extended its time in
session. During an average modern Congress members spend "275 eight-hour
days" in session (Davidson and Oleszek 1994, 31). Congress' workload has
doubled since the 1950s when Joe Martin was the Speaker of the House
(Davidson and Oleszek 1994, 29). This lengthened time in session reflects
Congress' efforts to deal with an increasingly more complex society.

As the Congress has produced more public policy it has also made
government increasingly more complex. Hugh Heclo writes:

> The late 1950s and the entire 1960s witnessed a wave of federal
> initiatives in health care, civil rights, education, housing, manpower,
> income maintenance, transportation, and urban affairs. To these, later
> years have added newer types of welfare concerns: consumer
> protection, the environment, cancer prevention, and energy to name a
> few (1995,265).

During these periods of great legislative activity, it can hardly be said that the
government has been in a stalemate. And certainly, the speed with which so
much public policy has been produced is little evidence that Congress has been
attempting to maintain the status quo. The increase in the production of public
policy, and the decentralization of Congress has seen the formation of sub-
governments[3] in which informal relationships have developed between
bureaucrats, interest groups and members of Congress (see Griffith 1939,182-
183). With the changing complexity of public policy, however, the cozy triangles
have given way to issue networks (Hugh Heclo 1995).

As policy has become more complex it has made public officials more
valuable to interest groups – not as representatives, but as lobbyists and policy
specialists. Members of Congress know the issues, and they have intimate
relationships with their former colleagues. One might therefore speculate that
interest groups might desire to hire former members of Congress to lobby on
their behalf. The formation of issue networks has led to the recruitment of
members of Congress to work as lobbyists where, many times, they can obtain
much larger salaries than by serving in Congress. Being that these individuals
are being recruited for their expertise, it becomes difficult to claim that retiring
members of Congress may be misusing their authority to benefit their future
employers. And there is reason to believe that former members of Congress who
become lobbyists are hired because of their expertise. Just as public policy has
become more complex, so too have members of Congress become more

sophisticated. Lester Milbrath explains that part of the reason former members of Congress did not become lobbyists in the 1950s was because the former members were not perceived as being particularly competent (1963, 67-68, see also Martin and Donovan 1960, 49-50). But this is less so the case today. The committee structure of Congress, in conjunction with the growth of legislative activity and legislative complexity, has improved the policy competence of members of Congress[4]. The improved policy expertise of members of Congress has made them more valuable to interest groups and lobbying organizations because, not only do these recently retired former members have close relationships with their former colleagues, they also have the understanding of policy and process that will give them credibility and success.

Others have suggested that the growth of the lobbying industry followed the New Deal and Great Society programs. Timothy Noah writes in Slate Magazine that the culprit for post-congressional lobbying can be found after the Great Society programs. The reforms that were enacted to diminish the role of big money on campaigns ushered in a flood of new contributors from the lobbying class. He writes:

> Previously, a representative could rely on a few wealthy patrons to bankroll his campaigns. Lyndon Johnson, for instance, entered Congress as the protégé of George and Herman Brown, who directed Johnson to secure federal contracts for their construction firm, Brown and Root. Once limits were imposed on contributions by individuals and political action committees, it became harder for one donor to "own" a representative the way the Browns had owned Johnson. But because each contribution was now smaller, House members had to devote more and more of their time to raising money. Today, fund-raising is a grind for all elected officials in Washington, but it's an especially dreary treadmill for representatives because they must run every two years.

> At the same time that campaign reform made being a congressman less enjoyable on a daily basis, it expanded vastly the power of Washington's lobbyists. No longer mere messenger boys for individual wealthy patrons, they became powers unto themselves as House members (and other Washington politicians) subcontracted to them the business of raising money. Increasingly, lobbyists came to represent entire industries rather than individual companies. The most successful lobbyists extended their fund-raising reach beyond those they represented and solicited contributions from the larger community of prominent wealthy people. In addition to rendering themselves more valuable financially, this mingling with the nation's elites raised the lobbyists' social status (Noah 2003).

The campaign reforms that resulted from the Watergate scandal improved the role of lobbyists. They were now a necessary part of the legislative process. They were now valued for the free information that they could provide legislators and for their fundraising prowess. Noah goes on to suggest that two additional events contributed to the desire of lawmakers to want to be lobbyists. The second major event was the further weakening of chairpersonships in Congress. He argues that once term limits were set on the number of years that member of Congress could serve as chair of one of the committees, the value of a chairpersonship was diminished. Noah writes,

> The time restriction dilutes a chairman's ability to master his role…
> Power abhors a vacuum. If House committee chairmen no longer rule
> with an iron fist, then who is left to define the terms of debate? The
> veteran lobbyist (2003).

The rule changes led to the creation of a chairperson who was constantly in training. Chairs are findings themselves essentially being demoted, or more recently, playing musical chairs – switching from serving as chair of one committee to serving as chair of another committee. Under this scenario, high-ranking and once powerful lawmakers feel compelled to leave the chamber to become lobbyists. And to encourage them to do so, lawmakers are witnessing their real dollar income diminish as they experience their retirement benefits improve after a short five years of service. Concludes Noah, "departing Congress makes more financial sense than staying there" (2003).

Public Policy and Discretion

But the competence of members of Congress does not dismiss the fact that they have discrete ambitions that can compromise public policy. Hugh Heclo points out that the increased complexity of public policy and the growth of government are further separating the representatives from the less technical public (1995). As the public becomes less able to comprehend complex public policy, it becomes easier for representatives to take advantage of this ignorance and sponsor legislation that they may not be held accountable for. This possibility is made all the more likely when members of Congress defer to committee and subcommittee members on policy issues on which committee members have policy expertise (Gilligan and Krehbiel 1989 and Krehbiel 1991). Even the congressional leadership fails to keep a check on the legislative goals of individual members of Congress (Parker 1992, 34-35). Individuals are granted wide discretion in Congress (Parker 1992). This wide discretion makes it possible for representatives to violate the public trust, especially if they are serving out their last term and the electorate is not in a position to punish a shirking member of Congress.

During the 1960s and early 1970s the Democratic Study Group contributed to the establishment of several major changes that have made the members much less beholden to the congressional leadership. The committee chairs would find themselves having their powers stripped away during this reform period. In 1970 the Legislative Reorganization Act, for instance, allowed committee members to move bills for floor consideration even when the chair disapproved. The Act also called for committees to publicly disclose committee votes. By the next year, the Hansen committee recommended that the party caucus be allowed to vote on committee chairs when at least ten members requested to vote. The "Subcommittee Bill of Rights" (1973) further tied the hands of chairs, allowing committee members to elect subcommittee chairs, rather than leave it to committee chairs to appoint people to such positions. The leadership, having its fate tied to the members, were then granted greater appointive and policy authority in 1973 and then again in 1975 (Rohde 1991,24-25).

The institutional changes that occurred during this time led to a change in the type of person who would seek legislative positions. Richard Fenno has suggested that the members of Congress were driven by a desire to create "good public policy" (1973). Others have found evidence that members of Congress tend to make altruistic decisions (Kalt and Zupan 1990). But Glenn Parker suggests that a change has come over those seeking public office in recent years. He suggests that members who once sought legislative office were driven by intrinsic benefits. He contends that Congress is now structured to benefit those who seek to profit from congressional service (Parker 1996). Congress has been structured to be more attractive to individuals seeking to profit financially from legislative service. Parker describes two ways in which the changes have made Congress more appealing to "rent-seeking" legislators. First, the decentralized nature of Congress enhances the ability of *individual* legislators to influence the content of regulation and laws. Second, the existing institutional controls on the avarice and discretion of legislators are exceedingly weak. These characteristics make rent seeking an attractive feature of congressional service (Parker 1996,75).

The changes in the operation of the House have led to a decentralization of authority which, on the one hand, have reinforced the Speaker's authority, while on the other, have made the speaker beholden to the members. This, in part, has had the affect of giving the leadership the power to take the lead on major public policy matters, while giving greater freedom to rank-and-file members to follow their own pursuits. As a consequence, there has been an increase in legislative activity in areas where there would be little conflict among members (Rohde 1991,32). Because of the committee's deliberative and agenda setting authority, members of Congress defer to the committee members on policy matters (Shepsle 1979; Shepsle and Weingast

1987). This deference to committee and subcommittee members in turn has led to an increase in the relevance of rank-and-file members in influencing public policy, which in turn has led to an increase in the number of individuals that interest groups find worthwhile lobbying. The division of labor, which arose out of the development of the committee system, has also led to the formation of policy subsystems – "patterns of interactions of participants, or actors, involved in making decisions in a special area of public policy" (Freeman 1965, 5). The division of labor, while improving the management of today's workload, has also made the committee relatively autonomous, leading to the formation of close alliances among committee members, bureaucrats and interest groups (Freeman 1965).

Members of Congress, as they develop expertise in their committees, often become policy experts. With the complexity of public policy, there has been an increased sophistication in the members of Congress. Charls Walker has written:

> In 1959 Secretary Anderson asked me to explain to a very fine and intelligent southern senator how banks created money and where that power fit into the monetary policy. It took a good half hour. Today most members already know the answer and, if not, can get a good fix on it from a short memo (1998, 26).

Walker goes on to suggest that the diversification of Congress has contributed to a greater understanding of political subjects, and this in turn has meant that elected officials – not their technical staff – are in control of public policy (1998, 29). As members of Congress have become policy experts, their expertise makes them valuable to interest groups and lobbying organizations that hire former members as lobbyists. Such personnel exchanges improve access and interaction between interest groups and Congress (see Fox and Hammond 1977, Haider 1974, 237-238, Hamm 1995, 295).

Congress has attempted to alleviate the danger posed by retiring members of Congress who may wish to become lobbyists upon leaving office by passing the Ethics and Reform Act of 1989, which placed a one-year ban on lobbying by retiring members of Congress. The intent was to close the revolving door which many felt permitted public officials to cash "in on their experience gained at the taxpayer's expense" (Carr 1996, 1517). But has the ban worked? The one-year ban went into effect in January of 1991. Since that time, there have been eighty-eight former members of Congress who have become lobbyists[5]. And this is not to say that these former members have stayed away entirely, only to return after the year has expired. Former Speaker of the House Bob Livingston did not waste any time in forming the Livingston Group shortly after resigning from the House. The Louisiana Republican, although barred from lobbying any of his former colleagues for one year, joined his former chief of staff Allen Martin and staff member Paul Cambon who are not barred from lobbying as they created a lobbying firm that would capitalize of the congressman's name and connections. The evidence suggests that the Ethics Reform Act has not achieved its purpose.

Conclusion

According to the Madisonian model, the electoral process should keep a check on the actions of elected officials. But, as James Madison was aware (Federalist 57 [1788] 1990,290), the check does not function when the member no longer seeks reelection. While this might not be particularly harmful to public policy or the representative process if the member intends to withdraw from public life without capitalizing on the congressional career, it is of great concern if the member leaves public life but remains active influencing public matters. The electoral process is not a sufficient constraint on the ambitions of members of Congress during their last term of office. While the framers did not intend to rely on the virtue of individuals to do what is proper, for a certain class of lawmakers, this is precisely what the political system has come to rely upon. And while Congress itself has attempted to remedy possible conflicts of interest by banning members of Congress from lobbying for one year, it has permitted sufficient opportunities for members to skirt the law.

The concern is whether members compromise the integrity of public policy for personal gain. Are they using their last term to reward those who may do them favors upon leaving office? One might speculate that there are such abuses of power. In their 1994 study, Herrick, Moore and Hibbing conclude that members of Congress develop more focused legislative agendas (225). While they applaud the last term incumbents for their focus, one might suggest that the focus is largely driven by the members' post-congressional ambitions. Members have many opportunities to influence public policy. They draft and sponsor bills and amendments, cast votes, and deliberate on bills in committee and on the floor. These different avenues allow members to have significant affects on public policy. And, as members have increasingly mastered their maximization of discretion (see Parker 1992), it becomes increasingly difficult to insure that members of Congress will not compromise the interests of their constituents.

In the final analysis, these issues become important because of the implications that they have for preserving or improving the legitimacy of Congress and other political institutions in general. If a political institution is to credibly regulate the conduct of its citizens, those very citizens must recognize it as legitimate. If this does not occur, then the citizens may deem public policy oppressive, and its implementation may be questioned. If citizens evaluate the institution by evaluating the conduct of its members, then the behavior of these public officials must be understood more clearly. If members of Congress are sponsoring legislation that compromises the interest of constituents so as to benefit future employers, then citizens may come to question the legitimacy of the representative and political institutions in general. If the legitimacy of political institutions is questioned, then this will have consequences for the democratic process.

---

[1] By making it difficult for majorities to form it becomes easier to safeguard the interests of minorities and individuals.

[2] For works that suggest the idea of iron triangles, see Cater 1964, Freeman 1965, McConnell 1966 and Lowi 1979.

[3] Sub-governments have also been referred to as iron triangles, cozy triangles, whirlpools and subsystems (see Keith Hamm 1995,290).

[4] Fox and Hammond (1977) describe how many members of Congress have increasingly had to rely on policy experts from among their legislative staff.

[5] The Center for responsive Politics has identified 138 former members of Congress who are working as lobbyists as of 1998, 64 percent of these, left office in 1991 or later.

2

The Context

When the framers of the Constitution set out to create a more perfect union, they were concerned that representatives would be gone from their districts for so long a period of time that they would lose their connection to their constituents. Roger Sherman, a delegate to the Philadelphia Convention expressed this concern most clearly stating, "The Representatives ought to return home and mix with the people."…"By remaining at the seat of government they would acquire the habits of the place, which might differ from those of their constituents" (Warren 1928, 242). This concern, at least for the better part of American history, would turn out to be unfounded. During the 18th and 19th centuries, members of Congress served relatively short periods of time. Many retired from Congress voluntarily, returning to their home states after serving for relatively short tenures[1].

Although it may have been the case that members of Congress were not gone from their home states long enough to lose their connection with their constituents, the short tenures suggest that congressional service and life in Washington were not greatly valued. Nelson Polsby reports that in the early Congresses, turnover was the norm rather than the exception. He writes:

> In the 18th and 19th centuries, the turnover of Representatives at each election was enormous. Excluding the Congress of 1789, when of course everyone started new, turnover of House members exceeded fifty per cent in fifteen elections – the last of which was held in 1882. In the 20th century, the highest incidence of turnover (37.2 per cent – almost double the 20th century median) occurred in the Roosevelt land-slide of 1932 – a figure exceeded forty-seven times – in other words almost all the time – in the 18th and 19th centuries (1968,145).

These early short terms are in part indicative of the lack of prestige that was associated with congressional service. While service attracted the well bred, it also attracted ruffians, and their antics lowered the prestige of the institution. Alexis de Tocqueville described the members of the house as "obscure individuals, whose names present no association to the mind; they are mostly village lawyers, men of trade, or even persons belonging to the lower classes of society" (1945,211). Men like Ohio's William Sawyer, Alabama's Felix Grundy McConnell and Tennessee's Davy Crockett were of this caliber. Their homespun plain-talk "produced lamentations about the decline of America's legislative branch of government" (Boller 1991, 28). Their behavior led to unfavorable and disdainful attitudes about members of Congress making government service less attractive (Josephy 1975,175).

Washington DC itself, was not a particularly appealing place to members of Congress. The first Congress to meet in Washington DC was welcomed by the dismal sight of three unfinished federal buildings – the President's House, the Capitol and the Treasury building[2]. When Connecticut Representative Roger Griswold wrote his wife Fanny, he described the place as "both melancholy and ludicrous... a city in ruins" (Green 1962,23). Senator Robert Morris wrote to a friend, "All we lack here are good houses, wine cellars, decent food, learned men, attractive women and other such trifles to make our city perfect... It is the best city in the world to live in – in the future" (Young 1966,46-50)[3]. This was a city that was hot and humid in the summer and cold in the winter. It was built on a "pestilential swamp", better known for its brothels and slave markets than for being the seat of government (Kilian and Sawlislak 1982, ix)[4]. It would be seventy years after Major Pierre Charles L'Enfant presented his vision of the city to George Washington that Washington DC would pave its roads, and even then it was in "rough cobblestones" (Josephy 1975, 187). Charles Dickens would call it a "City of Magnificent Intentions" with "broad avenues that begin in nothing and lead nowhere" (Josephy 1975, 187). The slow progress of the city's development made it less likely that members of Congress would continue to serve[5].

The completion of the Washington Monument in 1885, the Lincoln Memorial in 1922 and the Jefferson Memorial in 1938, as well as numerous public works projects that arose out of Franklin Roosevelt's New Deal policies, contributed to the development of the city's distinctly neo-classical character. And a new social elite began to arise in Washington. This new social elite combined the newly rich that could not work their way into the more established social circles of Boston, New York and Philadelphia with the political families that were increasingly finding themselves at home in Washington DC (Jacob 1995). Among those who entered this new circle of social elites were the former members of Congress who increasingly began to choose Washington as their home rather than Omaha or Des Moines (Jacob 1995).

Former members of Congress were now beginning to have good reasons for remaining in Washington DC after their tenure. Washington DC was increasingly becoming a city with the same stature of a London or a Paris. It was also a city with an increasingly active government with the potential to impact the private sector. This chapter describes the changes that the federal government and in particular the US Congress experienced from the time of the New Deal to the present. In doing so, three major changes in the congressional environment will be explored. The first of these will be the policy explosion that began with Franklin D. Roosevelt and continued to the present. A second major change that has occurred in Congress has been in the decentralization of Congress, which dispersed power to rank-and-file members – blurring the distinction between junior and senior members of Congress. And finally, these changes in the environment contributed to a lobbying explosion. These three changes in the congressional environment have set the stage for individual members of Congress to pursue their own policy agendas.

Growth In Policy

The US Congress has experienced two major spurts in legislative activity during the 20th Century. The first of these occurred with the New Deal programs, and was largely in response to the economic hardships brought on by the Great Depression and World War II. While the immediate intention had been to kick-start the economy, the long-term impact would be an ever-increasing role for the federal government in solving national crises. The change in the government's function was almost instantly felt. In 1930, three years before Franklin Roosevelt took office the federal government was spending 3.3 billion dollars – with less than a third going to non-defense spending (Barone 1990, 31). A decade later the federal government was spending 9.5 billion dollars annually – a 287 percent increase in spending. More than 80 percent of this spending would be going to non-defense programs[6]. The second major spurt in the production of public policy came with the Great Society programs of Lyndon B. Johnson's Administration. The Great Society programs, like the New Deal, attempted to spur economic and social equality. Both programs in the process gave the federal government new roles to play as well as a formidable growth in its powers. The end result has been the creation of Washington DC as a hub of economic and political power to which special interests must turn to receive adequate representation. As an indication of the growth of the federal government one need only look at the growth both of the federal budget as well as the federal register. The patterns not only demonstrate the growth of the federal government, but they also help explain the growth of the lobbying industry.

Figure 2.1: Nondefense Spending in Constant 2000 Dollars (1940-2004)

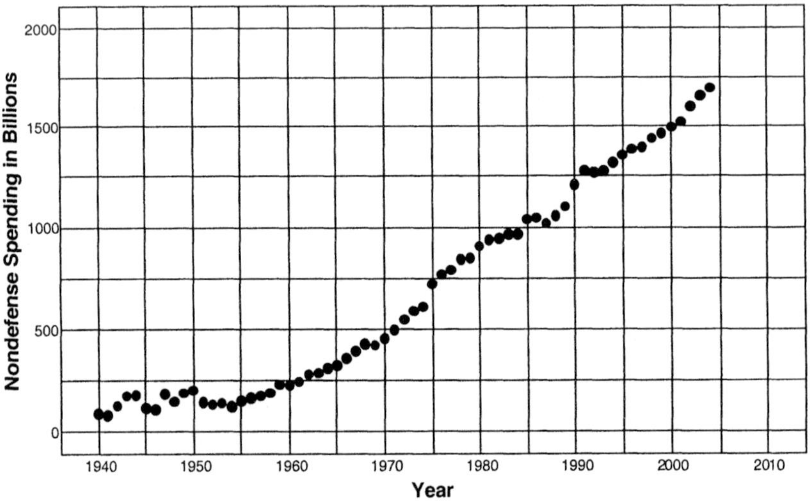

Source: Historical Tables: Budget of the US Government FY 2006

Figure 2.1 shows the growth of the federal budget beginning with 1940. The data takes account of non-defense spending and is based on current 2000 dollars. Looking at this figure, it is important to focus on the periods surrounding the 1940s and the 1960s. The figure indicates that the period following the Great Depression experienced a significant spurt in spending. To stimulate economic growth Roosevelt undertook massive federal spending. This increase in federal spending should have contributed to a growth in the lobbying industry as special interests went to Washington to lobby for their share of federal spending. But this did not occur outright in part because of the tremendous fluctuations in federal spending. The period surrounding the New Deal programs witnessed not only an increase in federal spending, but also a period of instability in federal spending. To make this point more clearly, we turn to Figure 2.2. Figure 2.2 shows the percentage change in non-defense federal spending from 1940 to 2000. The figure demonstrates that until the early 1950s, there were dramatic fluctuations in federal spending from one year to the next. In 1946 there was a 42 percent increase in spending from the previous year, while in 1950, there was a 31 percent decrease in spending from the previous years. Such dramatic fluctuations in spending would hardly be a friendly environment for the development of a new industry. By 1953 the fluctuations would become less dramatic clustering around an average growth of 8 percent, setting the stage for the development of the lobbying industry.

Figure 2.2: Percent Change in Budget from Previous Year in Non-Defense Spending (1940-2000)

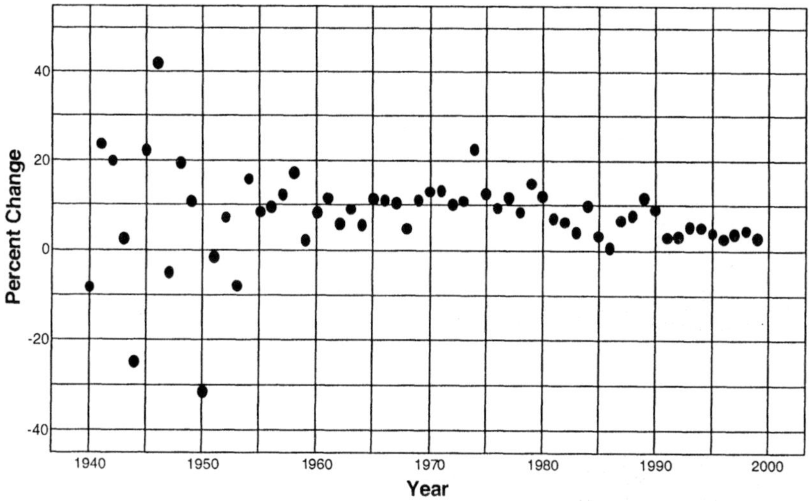

Source: Historical Tables: Budget of the US Government FY 2000

But stability was not all that was needed – so to was greater government spending. The Johnson administration would not disappoint. The period surrounding the later Kennedy years and the Johnson Administration witnessed a steady growth in federal spending that has continued to the present day. The gradual and consistent growth in federal spending can be attributed in part to the increased spending on social policy. Figure 2.3 shows payments to individuals that were made either in the form of direct payments to individuals or in the form of grants to state and local governments. It is here that the real difference between the Great Society programs and previous administrations is revealed. Figure 2.3 demonstrates that while there had been increased spending for individuals between 1951 and the mid 1960s, the period between 1965 and 1975 witnessed a much more dramatic increase in spending. This figure indicates that the Johnson years ushered in a more vigorous commitment to social policy than had been experienced previously. The Nixon years followed consistent patterns of growth in payments for individuals as those of the Johnson administration. Later administrations would experience slight fluctuations in spending patterns. The Carter administration, for instance would slow the growth of payments to individuals, only to see them resume under Reagan's first term.

Figure 2.3: Payments for Individuals in Constant 2000 Dollars (1940-2004)

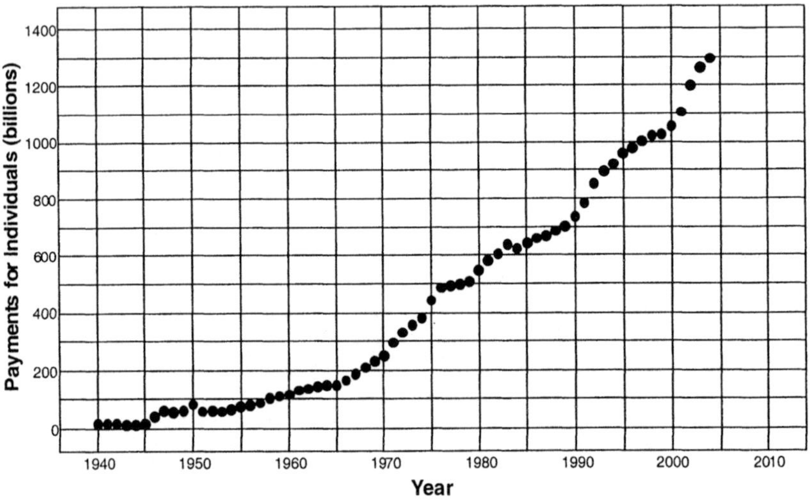

Source: Historical Tables: Budget of the US Government FY 2006

The growth in payments to individuals either in direct payments or in the form of grants to state and local governments has increased the role of the federal government, reaching more deeply into areas of American society. The more the federal government has reached, the more it has expanded its power. As the federal government has extended its reach and as it has more consistently spent public funds, it has created an environment that is conducive to a lobbying industry. But the federal government has extended its authority by more than simply increasing the size of the federal budget. It has increasingly been more inclined to encroach upon more areas of the public sector than ever before.

The federal government has become considerably more active than it has been in the past. If one simply counts the number of pages in the Federal Register – which is taken as a measure of the amount of federal legislation and regulation – one sees the tremendous growth since the 1970s. Table 2.1 presents the page count of the Federal Register for the years beginning a new decade. Since the 1940s there has been a gradual and consistent increase in the amount of legislative activity until 1980. In 1980 the size of the federal register grew to just over 87,000 pages. Just a decade before, the size of the Federal Register was slightly over 20,000 pages. This growth in the size of the Federal Register is indicative of a much more active federal government.

Table 2.1: Page Count of Federal Register

Year	Page Count	Change
1940	5,307	
1950	9,562	4,255
1960	14,479	4,917
1970	20,032	5,553
1980	87,012	66,980
1990	53,618	-33,394
2000	83,293	29,675

Not only does the federal government spend more and regulate more than it has in the past, public policy has become more complex. As discussed in chapter 1, the growth in the federal government has coincided with an increased complexity in public policy. Gone are the days in which US Government textbooks dedicate pages to the concept of the iron triangles in which friendly relationships between members of Congress, bureaucrats and special interests determined public policy. Hugh Heclo's issue networks have replaced such discussions. While in the past, friendly relations determined much, our more recent understanding of sub-governments call for policy expertise rather than cozy relations. Today's public policy is technical and knowledge driven. One might conclude that not only is there a lot more public policy today than in the past, today's public policy is also far more complex and out of the reach of most Americans. Given this environment, the lobbying industry places a huge demand on policy experts that not only know the players in the legislative game, but also understand the nuances of the law.

Growth Of The Lobbying Industry

With the consistent and gradually increasing growth of the federal government, the political climate was ripe for the growth of the lobbying industry. Special interest groups have been influencing the federal government from the beginning[7], but it has not been until well into the 20th century that the lobbying industry has become an institution in its own right. Its growth can be attributed to both societal changes and to institutional changes. From the societal standpoint, the growth of the lobbying industry and of special interests can be attributed to postindustrial changes, which have pitted one group against another. Loomis and Cigler write:

> Although it is premature to formulate a theory that accounts for spurts of growth, we can identify several factors fundamental to growth proliferation in contemporary politics. Rapid social and economic changes, powerful catalysts for group formation, have produced both the development of new interests (for example, the recreation industry) and the redefinition of traditional interests (for example, higher education). The spread of affluence and education,

coupled with advanced communication technologies, further
contribute to the translation of interests into formal group
organizations. Postindustrial changes have generated a large number
of new interests, particularly among occupational and professional
groups in the scientific and technological arena.

They continue...

Perhaps more important, postindustrial changes have altered the
pattern of conflict in society and created an intensely emotional
setting composed of several groups ascending or descending in
status. Ascending groups, such as members of the new professional-
managerial-technical elite, have both benefited from and supported
government activism; they represent the new cultural liberalism,
politically cosmopolitan and socially permissive. At the same time,
rising expectations and feelings of entitlement have increased
pressures on government by aspiring groups and the disadvantaged.
The 1960s and 1970s witnessed wave after wave of group
mobilization based on causes ranging from civil rights to women's
issues to the environment to consumer protection (1991, 20-21).

Social changes have contributed greatly to the development of interest groups,
but this is only part of the story. Just as society has changed, so to have the
political institutions which play a significant role in the development of society,
and Congress is no exception. While social changes were contributing further to
the promulgation of special interests, so to was Congress. The Legislative branch
and its scheme to regulate how public officials are elected and who pays for their
elections, opened the door to a flood of special interests that were all too happy
to assist candidates in their reelection bids in exchange for access to those public
official. Before continuing with how Congress has contributed to the evolution
of the lobbying industry, it is necessary to take a look at the growth and
specialization of the industry.

The lobbying industry has not only grown in the shear number of
groups that are now represented in Washington, so has its level of specialization.
The lobbying industry has evolved different types of lobbying groups, from
corporate interest groups to "boutique" lobbying firms that represent whatever
group is willing to hire them. Corporations, trade associations, unions and
membership organizations such as public and special interest groups have all
experienced phenomenal increases in representation in the nation's capital
during the 20th century. While for the first half of the 20th century it was virtually
unheard of for these different types of groups to set up headquarters in
Washington DC, this all began to change with the growth of the federal
government's spending and functions. Even as late as 1940, the number of
corporations with offices in Washington DC remained at five (Shaiko1998, 6).

But shortly after the election of President Eisenhower, "corporations flocked to the capital" (Shaiko 1998,6). The pro-business climate of the Eisenhower administration, in conjunction with the increases in federal spending of the previous administrations made Washington a place for corporations who could afford it, to open shop. Currently over 600 corporations maintain full-time offices in Washington, employing in-house lobbyists who represent and lobby on behave of the corporations that employ them (Shaiko, 1998,6).

As with corporations, associations and unions, which are organized around professional and trade membership, have also grown in number since the Eisenhower administration. In 1955, there were roughly 5,000 associations, and by 1996 there were 23,000 such national associations (American Society of Association Executives 1996, 1). Many trade associations tend to be organized around rather narrow special interests and thus tend to be rather small. The American Mushroom Institute, the American Wire Producers Association and the National Electric Sign Association are examples of such groups. Other associations tend to be much larger. The American Medical Association and the American Bar Association are examples of such groups.

Unions, like some of the more powerful trade associations are major political actors in Washington. While unions have lost a significant amount of their clout in recent years, there are several organizations that remain viable political actors[8]. The AFL-CIO, the International Brotherhood of Teamsters, and the United Auto Workers are three of the most prominent. The merging of the American Federation of Labor and the Congress of Industrial Organizations in 1955 created the largest union group in the Nation with a membership of 13 million. The International Brotherhood of Teamsters, with a membership of 1.4 million and the United Auto Workers with 200,000 members are also powerful actors in determining public policy that affects their members. Overall union and labor organizations contributed over 45 million dollars to candidates during the 1998 elections (Labor Force Statistics from the Current Population Survey 1999). And, while their contributions only account for 8.5 percent of the total contributions, labor has spent large amounts of money on mobilizing voters and issue advertising.

Public interest, single-issue and ideological groups have also gained greater representation in Washington than in previous decades (Walker 1983). Public interest groups have been in existence for some time. The National Audubon Society for instance was founded in 1905. More recently, the group Common Cause – founded in 1970 by former Secretary of Health, Education and Welfare John Gardner – has used grassroots lobbying to influence public policy in a variety of ways. Single-issue ideological groups have become key actors in influencing public policy and election outcomes. The Center for Responsive Politics reports that ideological groups have contributed over 36 million dollars to candidates (Center for Responsive Politics 1999).

If corporations, foreign countries, associations or other interest groups do not have the resources or need to hire in-house lobbyists, they also have the opportunity to hire lobbyists from a plethora of Washington DC legal and lobbying firms. These are lobbying firms that represent a variety of special interests. These groups have grown in number in recent years. The increased number of lawyers serves as an indicator of the growth of these *boutique* lobbying firms. In 1973 there were only 11,000 lawyers in Washington DC. One decade later, the number of lawyers had risen to 37,000 (Petracca, 1992, 14-15). Unlike in-house lobbyists, lobbyists-for-hire thrive from crisis (Birnbaum 1992, xiii). It is when a group is threatened that the group that does not have representation from Washington lobbyists consults with multi-client lobbying firms. In recent years, with concerns over tax increases, deficit spending and the unmanageability of national debt, the environment for multi-client lobbying firms has improved (Birnbaum 1992).

Lobbying organizations have not simply changed by increasing in number. They are also taking advantage of legal and technological changes that allow them to provide information and resources to members of Congress effectively and efficiently. Lobbyists serve as useful allies to members of Congress. They provide needed information that might be difficult or slow to obtain from the Congressional Research Service. At times, lobbyists assist in the drafting of legislation. While much of the information that lobbyists provide is technical in nature, they also provide information about the position that the legislators' constituents might take on certain issues. Lobbyists can use this information to pressure legislators or to prepare for public relations problems during election cycles.

Perhaps the most controversial resource lobbyists and special interest groups provide members of Congress is financial assistance. The 1.42 billion dollar "influence industry" contributes a sizable portion of the money candidates need to fund their political campaigns (Shuldiner, Allan, 1999). The one billion dollar plus congressional elections of the 1999-2000 cycle reflects an increase of nearly 25 percent since the last presidential election year – an election cycle when there were 189 more congressional candidates more than there were in 2000 (Federal Election Commission 2001). This increase in campaign contributions reflects an increase in the cost of running congressional campaigns. The Center for Responsive Politics reports that the average House winner spent over 800,000 dollars during the 2000 elections, while the average winning senator spent over seven million dollars (Center for Responsive Politics 2001).

Before the enactment of the McCain-Feingold, Bipartisan Campaign Finance Reform Act of 2002, The Federal Election Commission reported that 54 percent of the billion plus dollars spent by congressional candidates came from individual contributors, while roughly a quarter of the billion dollars was contributed by political action committees (Federal Election Commission 2001).

By 2004, 62 percent of the billion dollar congressional campaign contributions was made by individuals, while PACs made 29 percent of the contributions, and 4 percent was made by the candidates themselves (Federal Election Commission 2005). Of the 2000 PAC money, 75 percent was contributed to the campaigns of incumbent members of Congress (Federal Election Commission 2001). That incumbents are most likely to benefit from contributions only reinforces the idea that members of Congress have cozy relations with interest groups. Further supporting this notion is the fact that members of Congress receive substantial support from lobbyists and law firms. They are among the largest donors, contributing nearly 124 million dollars in 2000 (Center for Responsive Politics 2001). As the cost of campaigns continues to rise, so to does the dependence of members of Congress on campaign contributions. And, while the American people are increasingly concerned with the growth of the lobbying industry and the increased interaction between members of Congress and special interests, one might caution not to overlook pluralist theory, which states that the existence of interest groups helps to safeguard certain democratic principles. According to pluralist thought, the more organized groups exist, the more competition among these groups and the less likely that any single group will be dominant over other groups. Tyranny is averted because no single group can easily form to be the dominant group. From this view, a plethora of interest groups leads to· the protection of minority rights, and insures that diverse views will be permitted expression.

More important for the discussion at hand, one might be inclined to conclude that the American people should prefer the existence of many interest groups contributing money to political campaigns and lobbying their representatives. After all, would it not be better for a member of Congress to be beholden to a diverse collection of special interests rather than to a single group? Would not one prefer that one's member of Congress be beholden to environmentalists and industry, rather than just to industry or just to environmentalists? When members are indebted to diverse groups they are in a much stronger position to dismiss the narrow interests of a single group, than if they were indebted to a single group. If a member of Congress is indebted to a single interest group one might expect that the member of Congress be in no position to ignore the concerns of that group. The increased reliance on special interests, therefore, not only removes the burden of campaign financing from the American taxpayer, it also insures that members will not be as easily influenced by a single special interest.

The problem arises with the increased interaction itself. As members of Congress interact more heavily with special interests – either through fundraising or lobbying – members of Congress are given a greater opportunity to court prospective employers. One might imagine a member of Congress, not quite having reached retirement age, but thinking about leaving office, wondering what to do upon leaving office. One possibility might be to consider a career as a lobbyist. The retiring member certainly has the connections with other members of Congress that might help some group get its foot in the door. And, just as importantly, the retiring member of Congress also has the policy expertise necessary to become a lobbyist. One might therefore speculate that a retiring member of Congress might have a better chance of becoming a lobbyist upon leaving office if that member has a more diverse set of policy expertise. The significance of this hypothetical situation is that not only is it not hypothetical, but as we shall see, it is also been occurring with greater frequency.

Growth in Voluntary Retirement

Choosing to Leave

The focus of this section is on retirement patterns. More specifically, this section will describe the trends made by exiting members of Congress, as well as explain some of the factors that may have contributed to their exiting Congress. Figure 2.4 shows the number of members of Congress who have left since the 56th Congress at the turn of the century and up to the 105th Congress. Although the size of Congress has increased since the early 1900s, the figure nevertheless gives a good indication of the fluctuations in the number of exiting lawmakers. One can see in Figure 2.4 for instance, that the number of members of Congress who have been defeated in either primaries or general elections has decreased since the early 1900s. The number of members of Congress who have opted to run for a different office or who have been appointed to a different post has been on the upswing. In recent years, as many as 17 former members of Congress have left their existing positions to run for a higher office – usually their states' governorship. The number of exiting members of Congress who have received appointments to positions outside of Congress has declined since the 81st Congress (1949-1950). Before the 81st Congress there were an average of four members of Congress who received appointments. Since that time, 1.3 members of Congress have received appointments to other offices. If a pattern can be detected from the number of members who have been expelled or who resigned, it is that there has been little change. No significant increase can be detected. It is those who have retired voluntarily who have the most interesting pattern. To these we now turn.

Figure 2.4: Number of Members Leaving Congress by Reason for Leaving (56th-105th Congress)

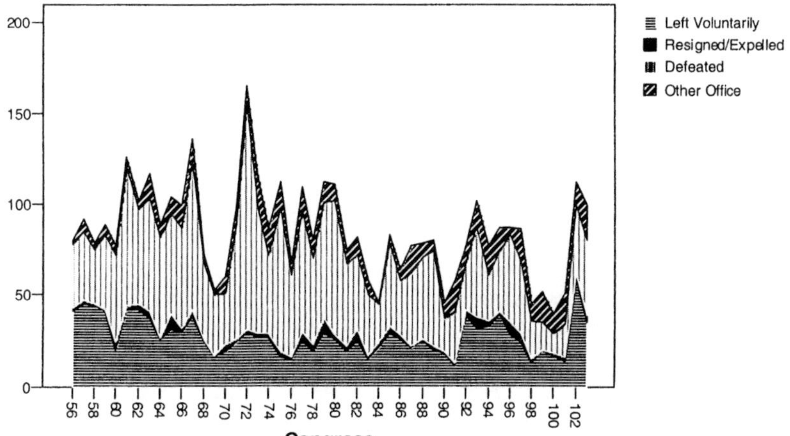

Retiring Voluntarily

In his 1968 work, Nelson Polsby argued that Congress was increasingly becoming more institutionalized (Polsby 1968). Among other factors, he took as evidence of this institutionalization the increasing lengths of legislative service as an explanation for his conclusion[9]. But by the early to mid 1980s, scholars were beginning to notice that the number of voluntary retirees was on the rise (Hibbing 1982a and b). Some speculated that the reason for this decline was in part do to the legislative reorganization of the late 1960s and early 1970s. John Hibbing, for instance, argued that the reorganization of Congress during this time led to disenchantment with congressional service (Hibbing 1982b). Increasingly senior members of Congress were not significantly more powerful than their junior colleagues, leading some to ask whether there was much to "look forward to?" (Hibbing 1982b). As the rank-and-file members were becoming indistinguishable from the more senior members, those more senior members quickly bolted out of Congress.

Figure 2.5: Average Length of Tenure of House and Senate Members who Retired Voluntarily (56th-105th Congress)

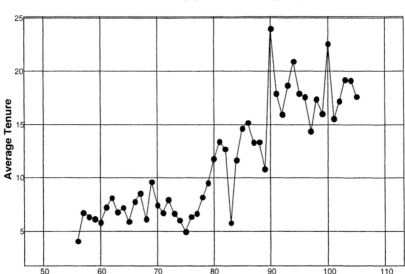

In Figure 2.5 one can get a sense both of the lengthening of congressional careers that Nelson Polsby observed, beginning with the 75th Congress (1939-1940), as well as the bolting on the part of the more senior members during the period shortly after the reorganization of Congress during and shortly after the 91st Congress (1969-1970). These two periods experienced significant decreases in Congressional tenures. The figure shows the average length of service of all members of Congress who retired voluntarily during this period. One can see from this figure, beginning at around the 75th Congress (1939-1940), members of the House and Senate were beginning a gradual increase in their length of service. This trend would continue until its culmination in the late 1960s, at which point the length of service of retiring members of Congress begins to level off, but not before the average length of service of those who retired from Congress reached its peak during the 90th Congress. Figure 2.5 demonstrates that the length of congressional careers remains considerably longer than in previous Congresses, but in more recent years the average length of tenure has decreased or leveled off somewhat. This *leveling off* pattern is similar in both chambers. Figure 2.6 and 2.7 demonstrates that after the 90th Congress, the average number of years served in both the House (Figure 2.6) and Senate (Figure 2.7) remained relatively high. During these later Congresses it would not be uncommon for many who retired voluntarily to have served 20 years in the House or Senate.

Figure 2.6: Average Length of Tenure of House Members who Retired Voluntarily (56th-105th Congress)

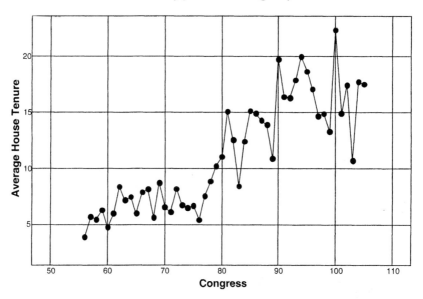

Figure 2.7: Average Length of Tenure of Senators who Retired Voluntarily (56th-105th Congress)

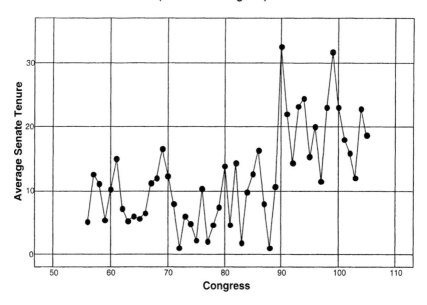

Retiring members of Congress have not only been leaving after a longer length of service, they are also leaving voluntarily in greater frequency. Figure 2.8 shows the percentage of all House members who voluntarily retired from the House from 1900 to 1998[10]. The figure indicates that early in the 20th century, the House of Representatives had a relatively high rate of voluntary retirements. In the 57th and 58th Congress, for instance, nearly a tenth of the House of Representatives left office. But these rates, almost from the start of the century, were beginning a gradual decline that leveled off between the 75th Congress (1937-1938) and the 91st (1969-1970). The 92nd Congress experienced a dramatic increase in the number of voluntary retirees from the House of Representatives. As Southern Democrats began to feel the pressure from fellow Democrats to become ideologically more liberal, many felt compelled to leave office (Hibbing 1982b). Others began to question whether serving was simply no longer any "fun" (Cooper and West 1981, Frantzich 1978, see also Moore and Hibbing 1992). The assumption was simply that members of Congress were opting to leave after shorter tenures because of the decline in importance given to seniority. Others however, have argued that perhaps more sinister motives have driven members to retire after shorter tenures – namely, that members were essentially being bought off. Changes in rules that allowed members of Congress to keep campaign contributions if they retired by the 103rd Congress, for instance, encouraged some to retire voluntarily (Borders and Dockery 1995, xiv).

The highest percentage of House retirees did not occur until the 102nd Congress (1991-1992). There are two explanations given for this dramatic increase – reaching nearly 12 percent of all House members. From one perspective, members of Congress were simply fed up with congressional service. Longer service was coming with fewer rewards and thus more members simply felt that the benefits of staying did not outweigh the benefits of leaving (Hibbing 1982b). Another explanation that is given focuses less on the disillusionment with service and more on institutional encouragements to leave. 1992 was the last year in which members of Congress could keep unspent campaign contributions for personal use. These incentives encouraged many to leave the House that year.

Figure 2.8: Percentage of all House Members who Retired Voluntarily (56th-105th Congress)

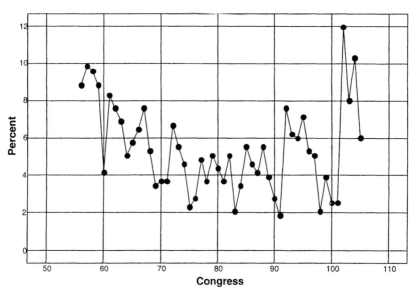

The Senate is a different story. Figure 2.9 shows that Senators did not experience the same patterns. Figure 2.9 shows the percentage of Senators who voluntarily retired from the Senate[11]. Just as in the House, the Senate witnessed high rates of attrition during the first few Congresses of the 20th century. But these rates quickly dissipated during the 66th Congress (1919-1920) through the 92nd Congress (1971-1972). With minor differences, the Senate, like the House, experienced increases in the percentage of Senators who retired from the chamber from this point on. For instance, while the House experienced a large increase in retirees during the 92nd Congress, the Senate did not experience that same high point until the 95th Congress – six years later. And, while the House experienced a sudden increase between the 91st and 92nd Congresses, the Senate – because of the staggered six year terms – experienced a more gradual increase to reach a similar high percentage of Senators opting to retire.

Figure 2.9: Percentage of Senators who Retired Voluntarily (56th-105th Congress)

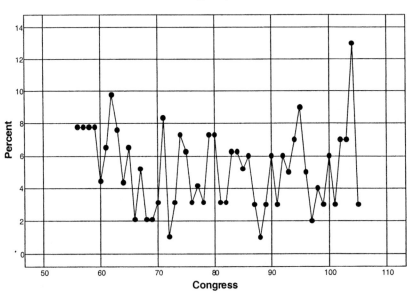

Catching Potomac Fever

With these increases in retirement, the number of former members choosing to remain in Washington DC upon leaving office also began to grow. Although data is not available for early periods, there has been an increase in the number of former members of Congress choosing to stay in Washington DC upon leaving office. Figure 2.10 shows the percentage of former members of Congress choosing to stay in Washington DC upon leaving office[12]. The data shows that the number of former members of Congress who opted to remain in Washington DC upon leaving office has increased in recent years. The years before the 1970s show that more often than not, former members of Congress were choosing to return to their home states upon leaving public life. But shortly after the turmoil of the late 1960s and the reorganization of Congress in the early 1970s, the percentage of former members of Congress choosing to stay in Washington DC began to increase precipitously.

Figure 2.10: Percent Former Members Staying in DC Upon Leaving Office
(1939-1995)

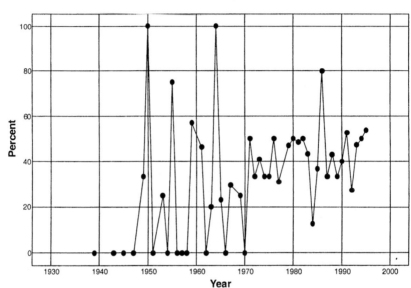

Increasingly more former members of Congress have been catching *Potomac Fever* – that ailment that has been striking public officials since the nation's founding[13]. Richard Fenno writes:

> It is conventional wisdom in the nation's capitol that senators and representatives "get Potomac fever" and "they don't go back to Pocatello" when their legislative careers end. Having pursued the goals of power and policy in Washington with increasing success, they prefer, it is said, to continue their Washington careers in some nonlegislative job rather than to go back home (1978, 223).

In an earlier study, I find that as many as 35 percent of former members of Congress who have recently retired have chosen to remain in Washington DC upon leaving office (Santos 1998, 44). If one were to focus on those retiring since the 1980s, the percentage of those staying in DC increases to 40 percent (Santos 1998, 43). The implication is that more recent former members of Congress are more likely to remain in Washington DC rather than return to their home states than those who left Congress in earlier decades.

Conclusion

The evidence shows that the number of former members of Congress choosing to retire voluntarily is increasing. This has been the case for the past several decades. This reflects a similar pattern found during the early 1900s, although in more recent years, the trend follows a period in which members of Congress were increasingly less likely to retire from office voluntarily. This more recent trend also reflects a period in which the rank-and-file members of Congress were given increasingly greater authority (Hibbing, 1982b). This loosening of the reigns in Congress, led to a diminishing of the value of seniority. And so, Hibbing posits that congressional service simply lost its value (1982b). But the more sinister view suggests that the increases in voluntary retirement are due to the increasingly "rent-seeking" nature of members of Congress (Parker 1996).

As congressional seats have become safer (Mayhew 1974), one would expect to find an increase in the number of former members choosing to retire rather than being removed from office by the voters. But what one might be less inclined to expect is the increase in the number of former members of Congress choosing to remain in Washington DC upon leaving office. Certainly, one might expect that as members are serving longer tenures, they are also retiring at an older age – an age at which they may be less inclined to purse a post-congressional career. But as we are about to see in the next chapter, the assumption – at least as it applies to the House – is not supported by the evidence.

---

[1] Between 1789 and 1801, 33 of the 94 Senators who served during this period resigned from office before the end of their term. (Congressional Quarterly Inc. 1976,182).

[2] Most members of Congress relied on the meager accommodations of boardinghouses, in which two members often shared a room (Carson 1990,138).

[3] The presence of so many men gave Washington a distinctly male tone. Englishman Frances Trollope commented on this subject in 1832: "There is another circumstance which renders the evening parties in Washington extremely unlike those of other places in the Union: this is the great majority of gentlemen. The expense, the trouble, or the necessity of a ruling eye at home, one or all of these reasons, prevents the members' ladies from accompanying them to Washington... Female society is chiefly to be found among the families of the officers of state (the cabinet), and of the few members, the wealthiest and most aristocratic of the land, who bring their families with them" (1904,192).

[4] In 1790, the founders of the District of Columbia planned to have the new seat of government, with all its grandeur, ready for its new inhabitants. The next year an auction was held to sell 10,000 lots. Only 35 were sold. A second and third auction did not fare much better (Jacob 1995,15). In 1800, there were 14,093 people living in the area, but about half of those actually lived in Alexandria and Georgetown. This was during a time when the nations' important cities could boast of populations of 60,000 and 70,000. In

1800 there were only 372 habitable homes in the city, leading some to speculate that had the members of Congress known what they had designated as their new capital, they would not have been so optimistic of its development (Jacob 1995,15).

[5] It should also be noted that as the nation moved west, the capitol was no longer as centrally located as it had once been. Some members had to travel considerably longer distances on harsher terrain than before. In order to deal with the long periods away with their families, more members were brining their families with them to Washington – the majority of whom came from Southern states (Jacob 1995,38). Those who did move their wives and children warned them to prepare to economize for Washington had little to offer (Carson 1990,139). It was only the very wealthy members of Congress who could afford to own two homes – one in the Washington area and a second in their district (Jacob 1995,26).

[6] In 1940 the federal government spent 9.47 billion dollars. 1.66 billion (or 17.5%) was defense related, while the remaining 82.5% was non-defense spending (see U.S. Government Printing Office 1999, 42)

[7] From the nation's founding the framers of the constitution were concerned that special interests, or factions would destroy the new nation. However, as has been discussed earlier, interest groups were incorporated into the political regime. For an excellent study of the relationship between corporations and the politics see Edwin M. Epstein. 1969. *The Corporation in American Politics*. Englewood Cliffs, NJ.: Prentice Hall.

[8] In 1983 20.1 percent of the labor force belonged to a Union. By 1998, the percent of the labor force that belonged to union had declined to 13.9 percent (Labor Force Statistics from the Current Population Survey. 1999. *Union Membership in 1998*. Released January 25. Internet address: http://stats.bls.gov/newsrels.htm.

[9] He also argued that the development of the committee structure further contributed to specialization – a further indication of the specialization of Congress.

[10] The percentages reported here reflects the size of the House.

[11] The percentages reported here reflect the size of the US Senate.

[12] Data source was complied from the addresses of the members of the United States Association of Former Members of Congress: Directory. This data includes only those members who joined the association.

[13] Historian Kenneth Bowling writes of Potomac fever afflicting the "Washington's and the Lees of Virginia, and the Johnsons and the Carrolls of Maryland" (1988,39).

3

Former Members of Congress as Lobbyists: Who Becomes a Lobbyist?

During the last several decades Congress has experienced a large increase in the number of former members of Congress who have either left office voluntarily or who have been forced to leave office for other reasons. Many of those who have left public service choose to remain in Washington DC upon leaving office. Because of the long tenures, many establish roots in Washington DC. For some, the choice to remain in Washington DC is determined by other factors. Some, for instance, receive executive or judicial appointments, which require that they remain in Washington. Some have even become disgruntled with their former constituents, thus making it difficult for them return home (Braun 1994, A-3). A significant number of former members of Congress however, choose to remain in Washington DC for the employment opportunities – namely for the lucrative lobbying careers that are available. This chapter evaluates the extent to which former members of Congress become lobbyists upon leaving office. The evidence suggests that post-congressional lobbying careers are becoming increasingly more common.

Figure 3.1 shows the percentage of all former members of Congress who have chosen to become lobbyists (post-congressional lobbyists) upon leaving office for each Congress beginning with the 93rd Congress (1973-1974)[1]. The figure shows a clear increase in the number of former members of Congress who have chosen to become lobbyists. During the 93rd (1973-1974) through 95th (1977-1978) Congresses the percentage of former members becoming lobbyists does not surpass 15 percent, but by the 96th Congress (1979-1980), 20 percent of former members are choosing post-congressional lobbying careers. In no Congress since the 96th has the percentage of former members of Congress choosing to become lobbyists been less than 20 percent. In more recent Congresses, the percentage of former members choosing to become lobbyists has surpassed 30 percent, with a clear upward trend beginning with the 94th Congress.

Figure 3.1: Percentage of Post-congressional Lobbyists by Congress

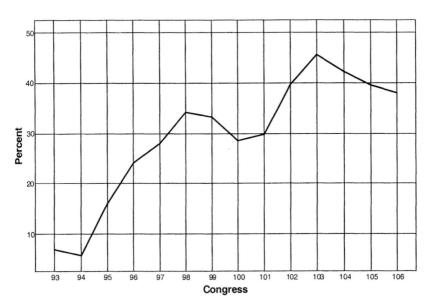

Given that Figure 3.1 includes all of the members of Congress who ended their service during the particular Congress, it perhaps makes more sense to look strictly at those former members of Congress who left office voluntarily – that is, excluding those who ran for a different office, received an appointment to some other office, lost their reelection bid, or who were forced to retire due to scandal, illness or even death. One assumes that members of Congress who choose to leave public life, rather than being forced to leave, are in a better position to prepare for their post-congressional career. A member of Congress planning to leave office to become a lobbyist may need time to plan such a move – purchase a home, inform prospective employers of such plans, inform constituents or fellow party members so as to prepare a replacement candidate. Of the 1,070 members of Congress who departed from Congress between the 93rd and 106th Congresses 407 ex-lawmakers left voluntarily.

Figure 3.2 shows the percentage of former members of Congress who have become lobbyists from the group of all who left voluntarily and who did not run for or were appointed to some other office. From this perspective, the distribution of former members-turned lobbyists is even more dramatic. The evidence suggests a variant, yet upward trend for those former members who have left office voluntarily. This figure shows that as far back as the 95th Congress (1977-1978), 20 percent of those who ended their congressional service would become lobbyists upon leaving office. With the 102nd Congress (1991-1992), the group of former lawmakers turned-lobbyists increased to 42 percent, and reached a high of 48 percent with the 105th Congress.

Figure 3.2: Percentage of Post-congressional Lobbyists Who Retired by Congress

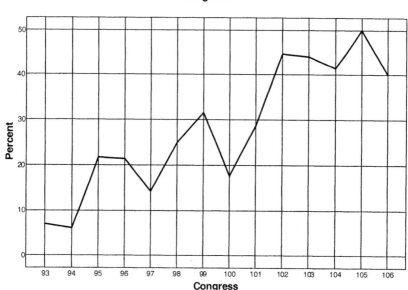

Figures 3.1 and 3.2 demonstrate a pattern of growth among post-congressional lobbyists that is reaching unprecedented rates. And in some ways it should be expected that former members of Congress should become lobbyists. Given that the lobbying industry is driven as much by friendships as by a firm knowledge of specific policy issues, it would make sense for the lobbying industry to court former members of Congress to come work for them as lobbyists. Former members of Congress develop strong relationships with their colleagues – relationships that transcend partisan affiliation. Interest groups, hoping to influence public officials would do well to recruit individuals that have strong relationships with members of Congress. It is not unusual, for instance, to come across registered lobbyists who have a spouse, parent, sibling or offspring serving as a member of Congress. It is also not unusual for former congressional and executive level staff-members to become lobbyists upon leaving their posts. These individuals have strong connections with policy makers. In the same fashion, ex-lawmakers have connections with policy makers.

Who Are The Post-Congressional Lobbyists?

Since the 93rd Congress, there have been 263 former members of Congress who have become lobbyists upon leaving office. These are the former members of Congress who are referred to as *post-congressional lobbyists*. These 263 post-congressional lobbyists are 25 percent of the 1,070 ex-lawmakers who have left office since the 93rd Congress. The likelihood that a former member of Congress will become a lobbyist does not differ between the two chambers. In both the House and the Senate, 25 percent of the members from each chamber become lobbyists upon their departure. Senators are no more or less likely to become lobbyists than House members. Interestingly, there appears to be some small differences between the lobbyists and non-lobbyists in terms of age and tenure. Table 3.1 below, shows the average age and length of Congressional service between the lobbyists and non-lobbyists in each of the two chambers. Among those who left the House of Representatives, the evidence indicates that those who become lobbyists are younger than those who choose not to become lobbyists upon leaving office. Post-congressional lobbyists are 3.24 years younger that the non-lobbyists. This does not mean however that lobbyists are any more or less experienced with the legislative process. House members who opted to become lobbyists have not served longer tenures than non-lobbyists. Table 3.1 indicates that lobbyists and non-lobbyists alike have served on average slightly less than 13 years in the House. For House members at least, post-congressional lobbyists leave office at a younger age, still too young for retirement, but experienced enough to capitalize on their post-congressional careers as indicated by the fact they have tenures as long as those of non-lobbyists.

Table 3.1: Average Age and Tenure of Lobbyists and Non-lobbyists by Chamber

	House of Representatives		Senate	
	Lobbyists	Non-Lobbyists	Lobbyists	Non-lobbyists
Average Age	53.21	56.45	60.98	61.8
Average Length of Tenure	12.95	12.87	19.14	17.26
Total (N)	(221)	(677)	(42)	(130)

In the Senate, there is an even smaller difference between the lobbyists and non-lobbyists. Post-Senate lobbyists on average leave office at the age of 61 while non-lobbyists leave at the about the age of 62. There is a slightly greater difference between the tenure of lobbying and non-lobbying ex-Senators than there is for House members. Former Senators turned-lobbyists on average will have served 19.14 years before leaving office, while non-lobbyists will have served 17.26 years. Unlike with House members, a slightly more experienced Senator is more likely to become a lobbyist.

Table 3.2: Percentage of Lobbyists by Party

	Lobbyist	Percent of Total	Difference
Democrat	51	55.5	-4.5
Republican	49	44.5	+4.5
Total	100	100	

Showing only minor differences are the members' party affiliation. The column labeled *lobbyist* in Table 3.2 shows the percentage of post-congressional lobbyists who are Democrats and Republicans. The column labeled *Percent of Total* is the percentage of Democrats and Republicans who have left office since the 93rd Congress. The final column reports the difference between the two previous columns. Of those who have become lobbyists, 51 percent have been Democrats, and 49 percent have been Republicans. Democrats make up a larger percentage of the post-congressional lobbyists, but, given that they make up an even larger percentage of all the ex-lawmakers who have served since 63rd Congress, Democrats are underrepresented among lobbyists. Since the 63rd Congress, 55.5 percent of all ex-lawmakers have been Democrats. Among the lobbyists, however, only 51 percent have been Democrats. Republican members of Congress, by contrast, make up 44.5 percent of all ex-lawmakers who left office since the 63rd Congress. Among the post-congressional lobbyists, Republicans account for 49 percent of the population. Given that 55.5 percent of the former members of Congress have been Democrats and 44.5 percent have been Republicans, Democratic post-congressional lobbyists are underrepresented by 4.5 percent and Republican post-congressional lobbyists are over-represented by 4.5 percent.

Post-Congressional Lobbyists and Committees

Many of the members of Congress who have gone on to become lobbyists are those who have served on some of the most powerful and prestigious committees in Congress. Those who have served on some of these powerful committees are in a much better position to get bills through Congress, or to help other lawmakers whom these post-congressional lobbyists will some day lobby for support from upon leaving office. It could be argued that these members are more likely to become lobbyists because of their connections with the current members of those same influential committees. Strong and friendly relations with members of Congress can insure a lobbyist great success in Washington. Special interest groups may, therefore, assume that retaining some of these former members of Congress, who have served in powerful committees, can maximize the interest of the group.

In the U.S. House of Representatives there have been as many as twenty-three standing committees since the 93rd Congress. While the names of some of the standing committees have been modified somewhat, for the most part these twenty-three have remained in tact. Table 3.3 reports the number of former House members who have served in each of those committees. Of the 897 House members, all but fourteen served on at least one standing committee during their last term in office. Of the fourteen, nine served as Speaker of the House or Minority Leader, and did not serve on any of the standing committees during their last term in office. The remaining five left office before they could be assigned to a committee. Of the 897 former House members, 610 served on at least two standing committees, 69 served on at least three standing committees, and five members of the House served on four standing committees.

In their seminal work *Committees in Congress*, Steven Smith and Christopher Deering classified the various committees from each chamber into five categories – *influence and prestige, policy, constituency, unrequested* and in the Senate *mixed policy and constituency committees* (199, 87,101). The first of these categories is the *influence and prestige committees* (1990, 86). Consisting of the House Appropriations, Budget, Rules and Ways and Means committees, these were described by members of the House as "important" and "powerful" committees (Smith and Deering 1990, 86)[2]. The evidence shows that House members who have served on these *influence and prestige committees* tend to be over-represented among the lobbyists. While 17 percent of all former members of Congress serve on the influence and prestige committees during their last term, among the post-congressional lobbyists, 23 percent serve on these committees. Because of the importance of these committees in getting legislation through the House, those who serve on these committees are in a position to capitalize on their friendships with other members who continue to serve as well as with those colleagues from other committees who made requests of them in getting bills through the chamber.

Smith and Deering identify a second type of committee – *policy committees*. Members of Congress see the policy committees as "attractive because the policy-oriented member seeks to contribute to the shape of important policies" (Smith and Deering 1990, 95). The House policy committees include Banking, Education and Labor, Commerce, Foreign Affairs, Judiciary, and Government Operations, while in the Senate they include Budget, Foreign Affairs, Government Affairs, Judiciary and Labor (Smith and Deering 1990, 87, 101). On average policy committees in both the House and Senate are equally represented among lobbyists and non-lobbyists. Just as 31 percent of all former House members served on these committees (32 percent in the Senate) during their last term, 30 percent of the post-House lobbyists served on these committees (30 percent in the Senate). It should be noted that in the House, policy committees are under-represented among the lobbyists, with one exception – the Commerce Committee.

Smith and Deering also identify *constituency committees* – those "with jurisdictions salient to their constituents" (1990,97). In the House these include Agriculture, Armed Services, Interior and Insular, Transportation and Infrastructure, Science, Small Business, and Veterans Affairs; while in the Senate these include Agriculture, Appropriations, Commerce, Energy and Natural Resources, and Environment (1990, 101). Generally, former House members who served on constituency committees are less likely to become lobbyists than their numbers would suggest. While 42 percent of former members serve on these constituency committees, they only account for 36 percent of the lobbyists. In the Senate, the ratios are relatively even. Just as 33 percent of Senators served on constituency committees, 32 percent of post-Senate lobbyists serve on these committees.

The last two types of committees are the *mixed policy/constituency committees* and the *unrequested committees*. In the Senate, Smith and Deering identify committees that are a combination of both policy and constituency. The mixed policy/constituency committees include Armed Services, Banking, Finance, and Small Business. These mixed policy/constituency Senate committees produce members that are slightly over-represented among the post-Senate lobbyists. While those serving on the mixed committees account for 25 percent of all former Senators, these same committees account for 27 percent of the post-Senate lobbyists. The last category of committees is the unrequested committees. As the name implies, these are the committees that members shun. In the House they include the District of Columbia, House Administration, Post Office, and Standards and Official Conduct, while in the Senate, they include Rules and Administration, and Veterans' Affairs. In both chambers, the percentage of members who serve on the unrequested committees account for 8 percent of all who served in the chamber, while among the lobbyists, 9 percent of the members served on these committees.

House Members in Committees

Table 3.3, shows the total distribution of House members who have served on the various standing committees. Column 1 shows the number of ex-members of the House who served on the various standing committees, or served in a leadership position[3], while the column to the right – column 2 – shows the percentage of all former House members who have served on the particular committees. From this, one can see that the Banking and Transportation committees have had the highest percentage of House members serve – accounting for 6.5 percent of all ex-members. Government Reform and Oversight has accounted for the least number of House members, accounting for 0.9 percent of all House members. Standards and Official Conduct and the

Washington DC standing committees, also account for a relatively small percentage of all House members, accounting for 1.5 percent of all House members. The evidence from column 2 demonstrates the relative popularity of the various committees. Those committees with relatively few members serving on them also tend to be considerably smaller than the more popular committee, thus reflected in the small percentage of House members who have served on those committees. Note that the committees with the greatest share of House members are constituency committees such as Banking, and Transportation and Infrastructure[4]. These two committees each account for 6.5 percent of all House members who have served on these committees during their last term in office. Vying for second place is Appropriations, accounting for 6.4 percent of all House members, while Armed Services and Commerce each account for 6.1 percent of all exiting House members.

Column 3, in Table 3.3, shows the number of ex-House members-turned lobbyists who have served on the various standing committees, and column 4 shows the percentage of all those ex-House members-turned lobbyists who have served on that particular committee. In column 4, the data shows a different story than that found in column 2. In column 4, three committees in particular stand out – Appropriations, Commerce, and Ways and Means. Members of Congress who have served out their last term on these three committees account for 25 percent of all ex-lawmakers who opted to become lobbyists, while only 17 percent of all the other lawmakers would become lobbyists. These post-congressional lobbyists are over-represented by 8 percentage points in these three House committees. The Commerce Committee is the single largest producer of ex-House members who become lobbyists upon leaving office – accounting for nearly 10 percent of all post-congressional lobbyists. Of the 94 House members who served on the Commerce Committee, 39 percent have become lobbyists upon leaving office. For the House Ways and Means committee, the second largest producer of post-congressional lobbyists – accounting for 8.3 percent of all post-congressional lobbyists – 42 percent of its members become lobbyists. The Appropriations committee, which accounts for 7.2 percent of all House members who become lobbyists, also contributes a large share of its members (28 percent) to the lobbying industry.

Table 3.3: Frequency and percentage of committees that lobbyist and non-lobbyist House members served in during last term.

Committee	(1) Total (N)	(2) % of Total	(3) Lobbyists (N)	(4) % all of Lobbyists	(5) Difference
Agriculture	87	5.5	17	4.4	-1.10
Appropriations	101	6.4	28	7.2	.80
Armed Services	96	6.1	21	5.4	-.70
Banking	103	6.5	22	5.7	-.80
Budget	60	3.8	20	5.2	1.40
Commerce[1]	94	6.0	36	9.4	3.4
D.C.	24	1.5	8	2.1	.60
Education and Labor	71	4.5	12	3.1	-1.40
Foreign Affairs[2]	82	5.2	18	4.7	-.50
Gov. Ops.	67	4.2	17	4.4	.20
Reform and Oversight	15	.9	4	1.0	.10
House Administration	42	2.7	12	3.1	.40
Interior and Insular	77	4.9	19	4.9	.00
Judiciary	71	4.5	10	2.6	-1.90
Merchant Marines	73	4.6	18	4.7	.10
Post Office	42	2.7	11	2.8	.10
Transportation and Infrastructure[3]	103	6.5	21	5.4	-1.10
Rules	31	2.0	10	2.6	.60
Science[4]	88	5.6	21	5.4	.20
Small Business	74	4.7	15	3.9	-.80
Standards and Official Conduct	23	1.5	3	.8	-.70
Veterans Affairs	66	4.2	9	2.3	-1.90
Ways and Means	76	4.8	32	8.3	3.50
Leadership	13	.8	2	.5	-.30
Total	1580	100	387	100	

[1] Commerce includes those members who served their last term in Interstate and Foreign Commerce (1947-1981) and Energy and Commerce (1981-present).

[2] International Relations has also been called Foreign Affairs (1947-1975, 1979-1994).

[3] Transportation and Infrastructure also known as Public Works (1947-1975) and Publics Works and Transportation (1975-1993).

[4] Science has also been known as Science and Astronautics (1959-1975), Science and Technology (1975-1987), Science, Space and Technology (1987-1994).

Column 5 shows the difference between the percentage of all House members who served on the particular standing committee during their last term in office and the percentage of post-house lobbyists who served on the particular committee. A positive number indicates that members of that standing committee are over-represented among post-congressional lobbyists. A negative number indicates that post-congressional lobbyists are underrepresented in this particular committee – the larger the positive or negative number the greater the over or under-representation of post-congressional lobbyists in the particular committee. In the Agriculture Committee for instance, one finds that House members who become lobbyists upon leaving office are less likely to become lobbyists than one would expect if House members from the agriculture committee were to become lobbyists at the average rate all House members.

What one finds in column 5 is that some committees produce a disproportionately large number of post-congressional lobbyists upon leaving office. With the exception of the Commerce Committee, the committees with the greatest over-representation among the post-congressional lobbyists are also the influence and prestige committees (Smith and Deering 1990, 86). The prestige committees in the House include the Ways and Means, which is over-represented among lobbyists by 3.5 percentage points; Budget, which is over-represented among lobbyists by 1.4 percentage points; Appropriations, which is over-represented by .8 percentage points; and lastly by Rules, which is over-represented by .6 percentage points. The two primary producers of lobbyists are the Commerce and Ways and Means committees. These committees are over-represented by 3.46 and 3.5 percentage points respectively. These two committees are over-represented by over three times the next most over-represented committee – Budget. What is particularly telling about the over-representation of the these committee members among the lobbyists is that these committees place the members in a position to assist other House members who are not members of the committee get funding for their special projects and to help the bill through the chamber, thus further ensuring that a bill or amendment will become a law. Having served on these committees, ex-members may be in a better position to ask their former colleagues to repay previous favors with better access, and even assistance on their own lobbying efforts. And, because these members served in the more powerful committees, close relations with the current members, further helps the ex-Congressperson lobby more effectively. This is all speculation of course. Finding evidence that shows that members of the more powerful committees are assisting their non-committee member colleagues with legislation is difficult to identify.

Senators in Committees

While the House of Representatives has produced lobbyists disproportionately from the more prestigious standing committees, the Senate, with its more diffused power structure, presents a different picture of lobbyists. In Table 3.4, as in Table 3.3, I report the distributions of all ex-senators and the committees on which they served, as well as the distribution of ex-senators-turned lobbyists and the differences between the two. There have been a total of 172 Senators who have left the Senate since the 93rd Congress – more so than in the more populous House, Senators tend to serve on more than one standing committee. Among them, the 172 senators have served on a total of 441 committees. Of these, the Appropriations and Foreign Relations Committees each account for the largest shares of ex-senators – accounting for 8.5 percent of all the Senators who have left office (see column 1). Reflecting the end of the Cold War, not only does Foreign Relations account for a relatively large share of the exiting senators, so to does the Armed Service Committee, with 7.6 percent of all Senators. This is the case even though these two committees – Foreign Relations and Armed Service – have traditionally, been moderately sized. Appropriations, on the other hand, accounts for a significant share of the ex-senators because it has traditionally been a large committee.

Of the 172 Senators who have left office since the 93rd Congress, 44 have pursued lobbying careers. These 44 Senators served in 111 committees. Column 3 shows the number of former Senators-turned lobbyists who have served in the various standing committees. Column 4 shows the percentage of former Senators-turned lobbyists who have served in the various standing committees. What is clear from the evidence is that former members of the Appropriations Committee in the Senate, similarly to that of the House, accounts for the greatest share of the lobbyists – accounting for 10 percent of all the Senators who would become lobbyists. Interestingly, the Senate Finance Committee also accounts roughly 10 percent of all ex-Senators who have become lobbyists.

While in the House, the powerful *money* committees tend to account for the greatest share of former House members who became lobbyists, in the Senate, this tendency is only partly true. While certainly, Appropriations and Finance remain significant producers of lobbyists in the Senate, so to are Judiciary and Small Business – relatively modest sized committees. Senators who have served On these policy and constituency committees tend to be significantly over-represented among the Senators. Column 5 shows the difference between columns 2 and 4. The greatest disparity among the committees occurs in the Small Business Committee. While only accounting for 17 former Senators[5], eight members of Small Business have become lobbyists. Senators who have served in the Small Business committee are over-represented by 3.29 percentage points. The eight Senators-turned lobbyists are 47 percent of the all the Senators who have served on this committee. The Finance Committee is a close second in terms of being over-represented. The difference between the percentage of all Finance Committee members and the percentage of Finance

Committee members who became lobbyists is 2.54. The Finance Committee members who become lobbyists account for 34 percent of all Finance Committee members.

When evaluating the over-represented committees among the lobbyists, we find that the greatest disparity appears to be in the policy and constituency committees. Unlike the House, where the members most likely to become lobbyists are the *policy generalists* who sit on the prestigious and powerful committees, in the Senate, the policy specialists who sit on the constituency and policy committees are the ones most likely to become lobbyists. This difference between the two chambers might suggest that the members of the House are wanted, not so much because of their policy expertise, but for their relationships with their former colleagues who serve on the powerful committees such as Ways and Means. The evidence from the Senate would suggest that the Senators who are most likely to understand the specifics of public policy are the ones who tend to become lobbyists. But this may be an overgeneralization of what is actually happening. More true to form is that the ex-Senators, by mere fact of having served in the much smaller Senate where members have a more cordial and close relationship with one another, can develop in the Senate the same traits that make House members valuable to special interests.

Table 3.4 Frequency and percentage of committees that lobbyist and non-lobbyist Senate members served in during last term.

Committee	(1) Total (N)	(2) % of Total	(3) Lobbyists (N)	(4) % all of Lobbyists	(5) Difference
Agriculture	28	6.45	7	6.31	-.15
Appropriations	37	8.53	11	9.91	1.38
Armed Services	33	7.6	6	5.41	-2.20
Banking	30	6.91	5	4.5	-2.41
Budget	27	6.22	7	6.31	.09
Commerce[1]	28	7.37	4	3.6	-3.77
DC/Gov Ops/Gov Affairs[2]	25	5.76	5	4.5	-1.26
Energy and Natural Resources[3]	31	7.14	7	6.31	-.84
Environment and Public Works[4]	20	4.61	6	5.41	.8
Finance	32	7.37	11	9.91	2.54
Foreign Relations	37	8.53	5	4.5	-4.02
Judiciary	30	6.91	9	8.11	1.2
Labor and Human Resources[5]	21	4.84	7	6.31	1.47
Rules and Administration	20	4.61	7	6.31	1.7
Small Business[6]	17	3.92	8	7.21	3.29
Veterans Affairs	14	3.23	3	2.7	-.52
Leader	7	1.61	3	2.7	1.09
Totals	441	100	111	100	

[1] Commerce, Science and Transportation also includes Senators who served in Aeronautical and Space Sciences between 1973 and 1977 – the year in which Commerce was combined with Aeronautical and Space Sciences.

[2] District of Columbia was joined with Government Operations in 1977, the same year that the committee's name was changed to Governmental Affairs.

[3] Energy and Natural Resources was previously named Interior and Insular.

[4] Environment and Public Works was known simply as Public Works before 1977.

[5] Labor and Human Resources includes those members who served in Labor and Public Welfare (1973-1977), Human Resources (1977-1979), as well as Labor and Human Resources (1979-present).

[6] Small Business was created most recently, during the 97th Congress (1981-1983).

Majority v. Minority

Members of Congress who left office while members of the minority party are more likely to become lobbyists than members of the majority party.

Figure 3.3 shows the percentage of majority and minority party House members who left voluntarily and either chose to become lobbyists. The first two columns show the percentage of non-lobbyists. It shows that the members of the majority party who opted not to become lobbyists exceeds the rate at which members of the minority party opted not to become lobbyists. The figure also shows that among the lobbyists, 30 percent of the minority House members would become lobbyists, while members of the majority party only account for 24 percent of the post-congressional lobbyists. The figure shows that members of the minority party are more likely to move into a post-congressional lobbying career than are members of the majority party.

Figure 3.3: Members of Minority and Majority Party Who Become Lobbyists

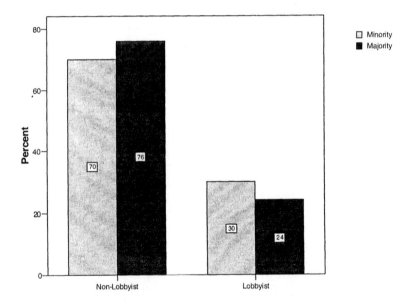

The discrepancy is not exactly due to the differences in age between the majority and minority party members. The average age at which both minority and majority members retire is 61 years of age. It does seem however, that minority House members who retire voluntarily tend to leave service after a shorter tenure. The reason for this might have been that members who are in the minority find it frustrating to continue service and thus leave office sooner. This hypothesis, however, is not supported by data collected by Rebekah Herrick and David Nixon (1996). In a survey of some 200 former members of Congress they asked members as to the reasons why they chose to leave office. Using their data, and merging it with my own, I find that among those surveyed, the rate of frustration between majority and minority members is insignificant. Figure 3.4 shows the percentage of majority and minority members expressing frustration as one of the reasons for leaving office[6]. As is evident, the data does not support the hypothesis that minority members are leaving office after shorter tenures out of frustration. In fact, the evidence would suggest that there is no difference between the frustrated and non-frustrated representatives.

Figure 3.4: Majority and Minority House Members Expressing Frustration

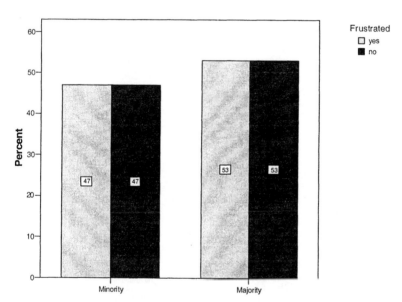

One possible explanation for the overrepresentation of lobbyists among the members of the minority party is that members of the minority party also happen to be disproportionately over-represented by members of the Republican Party, and as shown in Table 3.2, Republicans are disproportionately more inclined to become lobbyist than Democrats. While it certainly would not be prudent to speculate on the rent-seeking nature of Republicans, one might nevertheless explain the increase in former Republican Congress-members becoming lobbyists on the increase of political power of the Republican party in Congress. As Republican political power grew during the 1980s and 1990s, achieving a majority in 1994 in both Houses of Congress, the demand for Republican lobbyists grew. In recent years, pressure was placed on lobbying firms and special interest groups to hire more Republican lobbyists. As a consequence, Republican ex-lawmakers have seen their value as post-congressional lobbyists rise.

Congressional Leaders and Celebrities as Lobbyists

Increasingly, it is becoming a question of prestige for lobbying firms to have former senior members of Congress on their staff. Verner, Liipfert, Berhard, McPherson and Hand boasts the presence of the likes of George Mitchell, Bob Dole and Lloyd Bentsen on its staff of 185 lobbyists and attorneys[7]. Other notable lawmakers have started their own lobbying firms. The Honorable Howard Baker Jr. is one of the partners of Baker, Donelson, Bearman and Caldwell – considered the eighth most powerful free lance lobbying firm in Washington DC. It also boasts as its Senior Policy Advisor, Linda Hall Daschle – the wife of Senate Majority Leader Tom Daschle. Senator Alan Simpson who served as the Republican Whip from 1985 to 1995, quickly started Tongour Simpson Holsclaw Green LLC along with his Chief Counsel, Michael Tongour. Since leaving office Senator Simpson and his lobbying firm have garnered clients in the telecommunications and pharmaceuticals sectors.

Some ex-lawmakers who garner a great deal of national attention also get recruited by lobbying firms. This is in part due to the possibility that lobbying firms see ex-lawmakers as potential executive level government officials. Providing these ex-lawmakers with post-congressional employment establishes a firm relationship between the executive agency that the ex-lawmakers will soon be appointed to and the lobbying organizations that hire them. And this appears to be the case even though these ex-lawmakers are banned from lobbying for one year. Congressmen James Rogan and Daniel Coats are clear examples of this phenomenon. Congressman Rogan, the Republican Representative from California's 27th Congressional District and Assistant Majority Whip who gained national notoriety as one of the prosecutors in President Clinton's impeachment trial, was defeated for reelection in the 2000 general elections. Shortly after his defeat for reelection, rumors began to circulate throughout Washington that Rogan would be named Undersecretary of Commerce[8]. In the ensuing months he was brought on as partner at Venable, Baetjer, Howard & Civiletti, a prominent Washington Lobbying firm, which has a strong focus on intellectual property. Shortly after obtaining the partnership, Congressman Rogan was nominated as Undersecretary of Commerce for Intellectual Property and Director of the United States Patent and Trademark Office, by President George W. Bush. At the end of the 105th Congress Daniel Coats, the Senator from Indiana who replaced J. Danforth Quayle in the Senate, similarly joined a major lobbying firm in Washington DC. Senator Coats gained national attention as one of the leaders in the effort to shift power to the local level. Shortly after leaving the Senate, he, like Senators Dole, Mitchell, and Bentsen, joined the firm of Verner, Liipfert, Berhard, McPherson and Hand.

Senator Coats would serve in this capacity until his nomination to serve as Ambassador to the Federal Republic of Germany. These two congressmen are indicative of the type of former members of Congress that lobbing organizations and lobbying firms might be interested in recruiting. And, given that Government tends to recruit from within, it is understandable that a lobbying firm might see an ex-lawmaker as a potential member of the executive branch. From the perspective of the lobbying organization, having a strong relationship with a potential member of the executive branch would be highly prized. Lobbying firms therefore, would be wise to add ex-lawmakers to their staffs.

Whom Do They Lobby For?

Former members of Congress wishing to become lobbyists have a variety of choices of interest groups on whose behalf they can lobby. They can join some of the established lobbying firms. They can start their own firms. They can lobby for a single corporation, trade association, public interest group, single-issue group or even some other country. Figure 3.5 shows the percentage of former lawmakers who have become lobbyists by type of lobbying organization that they have joined. Clearly, the majority of lawmakers choose to join established lobbying organizations and law firms, with 53 percent of the post-congressional lobbyists joining such firms[9]. Interestingly, 32 percent of the members who become lobbyists start their own firms[10]. Eight percent of Post-congressional lobbyists lobby for trade associations. Five percent lobby for public interest groups and single-issue groups. Less than three percent of the post-congressional lobbyists are in-house lobbyists for major corporations. And about one percent is hired as foreign agents[11]. In this section I will describe the types of lobbying organizations that ex-lawmakers go to work for upon leaving office.

Figure 3.5: Percent of Post-Congressional Lobbyists Working for Types of Interest Groups

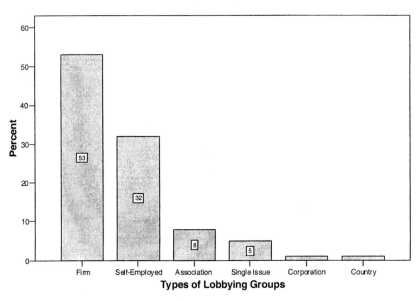

Types of Lobbying Organizations

With the growth of the lobbying industry, increasingly many law firms have developed lobbying and governmental relations departments. They differ from the lobbying firms in that they provide services other than lobbying. Law firms also tend to be more established than the lobbying firms. For the purposes of this study, I treat both law firms and lobbying firms as one type of lobbying organization. Clearly, firms are by far the biggest employer of ex-lawmakers. The firms that report having ex-lawmakers working for them have from one to as many as six post-congressional lobbyists. There is one exception – Advantage Associates. Advantage Associates has a dozen former members of Congress working as lobbyists. Advantage Associates is distinct not only for its large number of former members of Congress working for it, but also because ex-lawmakers began it. Many of the newest lobbying firms in Washington DC are the product of ex-lawmakers leaving office, and I report them separately in Figure 3.5. In Figure 3.5, the column labeled self-employed shows the percentage of former members of Congress who have started their own lobbying firms. These lobbying organizations started by ex-lawmakers rival the percentage of those firms that hire the ex-lawmakers. These new firms are able to achieve some success competing with the more established firms by attracting clients from groups that once lobbied them. Some lobbyists who begin their own practice may have no more than one client, while others, can have a very strong client base from the beginning.

The firms, both those started by former members of Congress and those that simply hire ex-lawmakers differ from other types of lobbying organizations in that firms will have many clients. And, while the firms may initially specialize in specific policy areas, they quickly broaden their scope to include more varied interests. A clear example is Dawson and Associates, which was begun in 1998, and between then and 2000, it has hired four former members of Congress – two Democrats and two Republicans[12]. The firm's founder, Robert Dawson, whose specialty is in the area of public works[13], has in a relatively short time broadened the firm's scope to include "water resource and natural resource management, environmental permitting, and regulatory compliance, as well as economic development, energy, defense, and government contracting."[14].

Most ex-lawmakers who become lobbyists do not lobby for a single-issue group. Corporations, trade associations, and single-issue groups do not hire in-house lobbyists from the ranks of ex-members. Part of the reason as to why these different types of organizations may not hire in-house lobbyists is cost. Effective lobbyists can be expensive, and keeping them on the payroll can be wasteful given that most interests are only rarely rallied into action. British American Tobacco, for instance was spending 160,00 dollars lobbying in 1997. In 1998, feeling pressure from state governments, it quickly turned to Washington for assistance, spending over 25 million dollars that year in lobbying. In 1998 it quickly increased its number of in-house lobbyists from two to three, and employing 40 lobbyists from a variety of firms – including former Senator Howard Baker Jr. and his lobbying organization[15].

Just as the Tobacco industry mobilized its lobbying efforts during a time in which its interests were threatened, many other industries also do not mobilize lobbyists until it is necessary. And, certainly one might speculate that some corporations will be reluctant to hire in-house lobbyists from the ranks of former members because it might seem unseemly to do so. Corporations, always concerned with the public's perception of them may be disinclined to hire in-house lobbyists who are former members of Congress.

Public interest and single-issue groups also tend not to hire in-house lobbyists. The data in figure 3.5 shows that these types of groups employ only 5 percent of the post-congressional lobbyists. And again, part of the reason for this may be cost. Post-congressional lobbyists are not only in a position to set the value of their services on the knowledge of policy areas alone. They can also set the value of their lobbying services based on the congressional connections that they have, thus making their services relatively expensive. These added values can make post-congressional lobbyists too expensive for public interest groups. Those members who do lobby on behalf of public interest groups, often times serve these groups out of conviction, more so than out of the monetary compensation that they will receive from lobbying on their behalf.

---

[1] The 93rd Congress is used a starting point in this chapter for two reasons. First; it is the first Congress following the legislative reorganization epitomized by three major changes in Congress. The first major change was the Legislative Reorganization Act of 1970, which gave rank-and-file members the power to bring bills to the floor in spite of the opposition of chairpersons. The second legislative change arose from the Hansen Committee, which recommended that the party caucus be allowed to vote on committee chairs when at least ten members requested a vote. And third, the 1973 "Subcommittee Bill of Rights" further constrained the chairs' power to appoint subcommittee chairs. These three changes have empowered the rank-and-file members, leading to a revolution in the way Congress has operated from that point on. The second reason for starting with 1973 deals with availability of data. Data identifying former members of Congress who have become lobbyists is not readily available until the 1970s.

[2] Smith and Deering only identify House committees as being influence and prestige committees. Smith and Deering admit, "Members goals are less easily characterized in the Senate than in the House" (1990,100).

[3] See the second to the last row in table 3.3.

[4] Previously known as *Public Works*.

[5] The Small Business Committee is a relatively new committee, having been created in during the 97th Congress (1981-1983).

[6] In order to maximize the use of the survey data, I include all those members who answered the survey, which includes 196 members of the House of Representatives and 11 Senators.

[7] See "The Influence Merchants" *Fortune*. December 7, 1998.

[8] Glendale. 2001. "Southern California News Briefs; Former Congressman Lands Washington Job" *Los Angeles Times*. March 3. Metro Section Part B Page 10.

[9] It is important to distinguish between established and not established lobbying firms, given that many ex-lawmakers start their own lobbying firms.

[10] The number of post-congressional lobbyists who began their own lobbying firms was determined by matching the name of the ex-lawmaker with the name of the firm they were lobbying firm.

[11] It should be noted that most countries that lobby the United States hire lobbying firms to represent their interests.

[12] The four are Democrats Tom Bevill of Alabama and Ronald Packard of California, and Republicans Jan Meyers of Kansas and John Myers of Indiana.

[13] McAllister, Bill. 1998. "Comsat's Heavy Hitters". *The Washington Post*. January 8. Section A, Pg. 19.

[14] Home page of Dawson and Associates. http://www.dawsonassociates.com

[15] Data source: Center for Responsive Politics, http://www.opensecrets.org.

4

Sending Signals Or Rewarding Future Employers With Bill Sponsorship

The focus of this chapter and the coming chapter will be on whether former lawmakers reward their future employers with public policy. This chapter will take a more quantitative approach, while the following chapter will take a more qualitative approach to demonstrating the connection between lawmakers, the policy they support, and the groups that they eventually go to work for. This chapter will focus on the ways in which the behavior of House and Senate members who become lobbyists changes as they approach their exit from Congress, and how that change differs from the behavior of the their colleagues who do not become lobbyists. It is suspected that some exiting members of Congress will attempt to position themselves for careers as lobbyists. One possibility is that the exiting lawmakers may attempt to advertise their employment eligibility by sending signals to their prospective employers. Members of Congress, hoping to become lobbyists, may feel the need to advertise their skills by introducing bills during their last term in office. By submitting a large number of bills on a particular subject lawmakers send the signal to the broader community that they are experts in those particular policy areas. A member may also attempt to demonstrate robustness by submitting lots of bills. Being active legislatively could be construed to mean being vibrant and engaged – characteristics valued by some employers. Others may focus on policy areas that they have sincere passions about, and could conceivably want to demonstrate those passions as they retire from Congress. Given these possibilities, it is conceivable that exiting members of Congress may simply be sending signals to the special interest community.

A more nefarious explanation as to why members of Congress remain legislatively active as they are approaching the end of their congressional careers is that they are actually rewarding their future employers before they leave

Congress. If this were so, one would not simply expect to see members who plan to become lobbyists submitting lots of bills. One might expect these members of Congress to be successful at getting their bills out of committee and to the floor. One might also expect these bills to make it to the other chamber, and perhaps to the President's desk. If these actions were to happen the retiring members of Congress would be doing far more than simply sending signals. They would actually be working diligently to get the bills enacted into law. Furthermore, one would expect to see these laws having a direct and positive impact on the interest group or groups that the retiring members of Congress plan to work for upon leaving office. Exiting lawmakers may be rewarding their future employers with minor regulatory changes or support with unpopular policy positions. If ex-lawmakers are taking legislative action that benefits them directly, then the appropriateness of such legislative actions may violate the members' code of conduct.

It is these two concerns – whether members of Congress are sending signals, or rewarding the interest groups that they plan to work for with public policy – that are the focus of this chapter. The evidence will show that those lawmakers who become lobbyists upon leaving office behave differently during their last legislative session compared to those who do not become lobbyists. Not only do they submit more bills during their last session, they are also more likely to get these bills enacted into law.

Sending Signals with Bills

The question of whether members of Congress send signals with public policy is nothing new. Members of Congress have used their positions to send signals to industry, special interest groups and their constituents since the beginning of the Republic. They send signals in a variety of ways. Members can give speeches on the House floor, in their home districts, or before special interest groups. They can also use their franking privileges to send letters to their constituents, informing them of what the member of Congress has done or plans to do. Members of Congress can write to local or national newspapers, or make appearances on television. Lawmakers can also send signals by sponsoring or cosponsoring bills. Even knowing that these bills have a very small chance of becoming law, Congress-members will sponsor legislation simply to send signals. David Mayhew quotes a member of Congress as saying that he sponsors bills so as to be able to take credit for the sponsorship of such bills (Mayhew 1974, 63, fn).

What is less clear is whether signaling occurs as the lawmakers serve their last term in office, and why they may do so. Members of Congress planning their exit from the House may attempt to demonstrate policy expertise by sending signals to the world at-large. Some have found that during this last term in office, departing members of Congress take on a more daring agenda

(Jacobson 1992). Some have even suggested that once the electorate is no longer relevant – i.e. during the last term in office – the agenda becomes more "focused and potentially successful" (Herrick, Moore and Hibbing 1994, 225). Once constituents no longer matter, retiring lawmakers are free to sponsor bills without the fear of their constituents. Among these lawmakers planning their leave from public life, one might expect that many will be seeking post-congressional employment. One might expect that some of these lawmakers may want to advertise their expertise by sending signals to one major set of employers – lobbying firms. I hypothesize, therefore, that these lawmakers will want to send signals to their possible employers. Departing lawmakers may sponsor bills to get the attention of special interest groups. They may do this for the purpose of demonstrating policy expertise and to indicate that they are available for employment.

I begin by asking whether there is a difference in bill sponsorship between lawmakers who become lobbyists and those who do not become lobbyists. What I find is that those lawmakers who become lobbyists do in fact remain active during their last term in office, while those who do not become lobbyists slow down their legislative activity during their last term. Of 659 House members who served at least two consecutive terms between 1976 and 2000, those who would become lobbyists remained significantly more active than their counterparts who did not become lobbyists. To measure this difference, I subtracted the number of bills introduced by House members during the penultimate session from the last session in which these exiting members served. Figure 4.1 shows these differences between the lobbyists and non-lobbyists. I found that the soon to be lobbyists slightly increased their pace of legislative activity, i.e. the number of bills sponsored. The average difference in the number of bills sponsored from one Congress to the next was a modest 35 percent of a bill. That is to say, there was an *increase* of a third of a bill being sponsored by post-congressional lobbyists from the post-congressional lobbyists' previous term. Among those who opted not to become lobbyists, there was an average *decrease* in bill sponsorship of 3.69 bills.

Figure 4.1: Differences in Bill Sponsorship in the House. Lobbyists and Non-Lobbyists 1976-2000

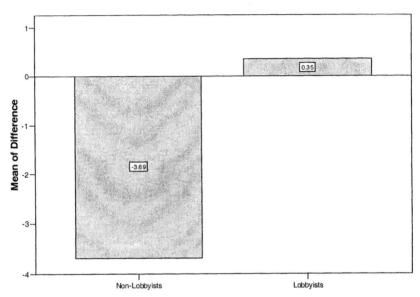

Although not shown, lawmakers who become lobbyists are less active than their counterparts who do not become lobbyists during their penultimate session. Post-congressional lobbyists have a history of being less active[1]. During the second to the last Congress, those who do not become lobbyists are more active than their lobbying counterparts – on average introducing 22 bills compared to the 18 bills introduced by the future lobbyists during the same time period. Among the soon to be lobbyists, those making up the top 5 percent of bill sponsors average only 68 bills each during the penultimate Congress, while the top 5 percent of bill sponsors who do not become lobbyists average 110 bills during their penultimate session. Ex-lawmakers who eventually become lobbyists have a history of being less active than their non-lobbyist counterparts. Their non-lobbyist counterparts change dramatically when they serve their last term, while those who become lobbyists change little.

In a more rigorous analysis, I have found that the number of bills sponsored by a retiring lawmaker can be explained by two factors – the number of bills that they sponsored during their penultimate term in Congress, and whether the lawmaker chooses a lobbying career or not upon leaving office. Those who become lobbyists sponsor more bills than those who do not become lobbyists. In some instances, those who were less active during their penultimate term actually became more active as they prepared to leave office to become lobbyists (Santos 2003, Santos 2004). The relationship between the number of bills sponsored and the post-congressional career choice is further strengthened when controlling for the manner in which the lawmakers left office. In the 2004 study, I controlled for three ways in which retiring lawmakers might depart – *having been defeated for reelection, having sought a higher office,* and *having left voluntarily.* Those who were defeated for reelection or who sought a higher office and lost, were not in a position to prepare for their post-congressional careers as lobbyists. As such, among those who lost their reelection bid or who sought a higher office there is no difference in the number of bills sponsored between those who became lobbyists and those who did not become lobbyists (Santos 2004). It is only among those who left voluntarily that there is a strong relationship between bill sponsorship and post-congressional lobbying (Santos 2004). Those who become lobbyists after having volunteered to leave are the lawmakers most likely to remain active sponsoring bills during their final term in office. Figure 4.2 shows the difference between the number of bills sponsored by lobbyists and non-lobbyists, controlling for the reason why they left the Congress. A negative number would indicate that the lobbyists sponsored fewer bills than the non-lobbyists for each of the categories. A positive number would indicate that the lobbyists sponsored more bills than the non-lobbyists. Figure 4.2 indicates that it is only among those ex-lawmakers who retired voluntarily that we see a positive increase in the number of bills sponsored by lobbyists. Compared to lawmakers who are defeated in general or primary elections, were appointed to or ran for some other office, or resigned, voluntary retirees who lobby sponsor more bills than those who do not lobby – a difference of 1.01 bills. Voluntary retirees may be better situated to plan to leave office years before they actually do. As a result, they are better able to plan their exit from Congress with an understanding of where they would like to be employed after their service. These lawmakers who plan their retirement are preparing a soft landing for themselves upon leaving office. Those post-congressional lobbyists who are forced out of Congress without much time to plan their exit, by contrast were less likely to increase their legislative activity during their last term.

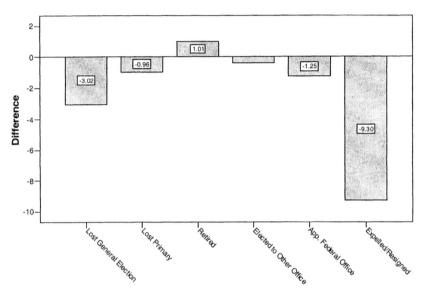

Figure 4.2: Differences in Bill Sponsorship in House and Senate Controlling for Reason for Leaving Congress.

Why Are Ex-Lawmakers Wanted? Three Hypotheses

Why are ex-lawmakers wanted as lobbyists? While there may be as many answers to this question as there are ex-lawmakers seeking post-congressional lobbying careers, many of the possible explanations to the question can be grouped into three categories. Post-congressional lobbyists have *policy expertise*, *procedural expertise*, and *contacts*. The first explanation is that lawmakers are wanted as lobbyists because they know public policy better than most people including other lobbyists. As was described in the beginning of the book, public policy has become extremely complex and thus difficult for laypeople to understand. It takes very intelligent, knowledgeable people who know public policy very well to lobby for or against certain initiatives. Lawmakers fit this description well. Lawmakers are much better educated than the average American, and they have been intimately involved in the creation of a significant portion of modern public policy. A second answer to the question is that they know the process. Perhaps more important than knowing public policy is to know how policy is created. The policy process is far more intricate and cumbersome than the textbook explanation of how a bill becomes a law. It is not enough to know the orthodoxies of lawmaking. Just as valuable is to know the unwritten steps to creating or preventing the creation of public policy.

Lawmakers are also wanted as lobbyists because they know the "right people". They not only know the "right people", they are friends and colleagues of the "right the people". The right people of course are other lawmakers and their aides, members of the executive branch, and bureaucrats.

Policy Expertise

"I sell what I know." This is how the former Senator from Minnesota, Dave Durenberger, describes what he does as a lobbyist for APCO Associates (Eilperin 1996). A special interest firm that represents the medical industry would be wise to hire an ex-lawmaker like Senator Durenberger who once served on the Special Committee on Aging. Former Congress member William Ford similarly echoes this sense of the importance of knowledge when he states, "I accumulate all of that knowledge in my mental computer and spit out wisdom" (Eilperin 1996). Rank-and-file members of Congress have increasingly accumulated this wisdom. With the decentralization of Congress in the 1970s, power was increasingly diffused throughout the chamber. Beginning in the early 1970s, every lawmaker was a source of political power and thus worth lobbying. The Civil Rights Movement, Vietnam, and Watergate – all contributed to a redistribution of political power away from the presidency, and placed it in Congress. Congress, in turn reorganized itself. It moved away from the seniority and apprenticeship systems, which had developed. The seniority system rewarded the most senior members of Congress with chairpersonships of congressional committees, while apprenticeships gave new members the opportunity to develop expertise as more senior lawmakers mentored them. As the seniority and apprenticeship systems were devalued, the rank-and-file members of Congress now had more autonomy than they had ever had before. This increased autonomy came as members of Congress moved to be more open than they had ever been before. Thomas Hale Boggs, the son of two members of Congress and Senior Partner with the lobbying firm Patton Boggs, describes what resulted from these changes this way:

> When they did things behind closed doors—you know, "I'll vote for your levee in Louisiana if you vote for my potato crop in Vermont"— there was no rationale to that. It was a buddy system and a leadership system. And all of a sudden they were before God and cameras and they had to justify why they're from Vermont voting for a levee in Louisiana. So they didn't vote for it. And that also did something else. It created a great desire on their part for information. They didn't have to shine before. Now even the old guard had to look smart. It created a great demand for information, which probably changed the system more than anything else. And that information also became something that special interests learned they could

develop quicker, better, faster, and more accurately than the government could (Center for Public Integrity 1997b).

As lawmakers searched for information they relied on lobbyists. And as they acquired this information, lawmakers became experts in their respective arenas. The decentralization of Congress made all members of Congress policy experts. For many, by the time they would leave office knew as much if not more than many of those lobbying them. The next logical step for a retiring lawmaker not quite ready for retirement and having accumulated so much information was the lobbying arena.

Given their experience and knowledge, it would be rational for lobbying firms and special interest groups to employ ex-lawmakers like Durenberger as lobbyists. A firm lobbying on behalf of agriculture might be inclined to hire ex-lawmakers who served in the House Agriculture Committee, while a special interest seeking a lobbyist with familiarity in education might seek to hire a lobbyist who comes out of the committee overseeing education. It is committees like these – education, agriculture, and banking – that produce some of the most well informed experts with very specific and narrow policy area concentrations. But are policy experts, i.e. those who developed their expertise in the policy committees, the ones most likely to become lobbyists? One way of testing for the value of policy expertise is to look at the extent to which former members of Congress who become lobbyists come from those committees that serve particular constituents or policy areas where policy expertise can be obtained. While it is clear that these committees do in fact produce lobbyists, they do so at a lower rate than committees that provide members of Congress power rather than expertise. Those most likely to find employment as lobbyists upon leaving office are those who served on the most powerful committees. That is to say, those who become lobbyists are not necessarily the members of Congress who served on the policy committees that would allow the member of Congress to become highly specialized in a particular field like agriculture or education. Looking at the House, the only policy committee that produces a large number of lobbyists is Energy and Commerce. This is an observation that has been made by others as well.

> We found that the revolving door practically came unhinged on some of the "money" committees, such as the Senate and House Commerce Committees, where 36 and 40 percent of senior staffers there, respectively, left to become registered lobbyists. So if you ever wonder why the lobbyists who ply their trade on Capitol Hill are so effective and so highly compensated, remember the numbers—they are true insiders (Lewis 1998, 2).

Of the 94 former House members who have served on Energy and Commerce during the period under investigation, 36 have become lobbyists.

Generally, those who become lobbyists have a higher tendency to have come from the more general and more powerful committees like Appropriations, Budget and Ways and Means. Figure 4.3 shows the percentage of members in the four prestige committees that have become lobbyists since the mid 1970s. Ways and Means appears to be a "lobbyist" factory, turning nearly half of its members into lobbyists. Forty-two percent of those who have served on Ways and Means during the period under investigation have become lobbyists. Also producing a sizeable percentage of lobbyists from its ranks are the other three powerful committees. It should be noted however that Rules and to a lesser extent Budget have traditionally been smaller committees with fewer members. As a consequence, while 32 percent of the members in Rules have become lobbyists, that is only 10 of 31 members who have become lobbyists. Similarly, 33 percent of the members serving on Budget have become lobbyists. The 33 percent reflects 20 out of 60 members who have served on that committee and become lobbyists. Appropriations, however, is one of the largest committees having produced 101 former House members. Of these 101 former members 28 have become lobbyists.

Figure 4.3: Percent of House Members from Prestige Committees who Lobby

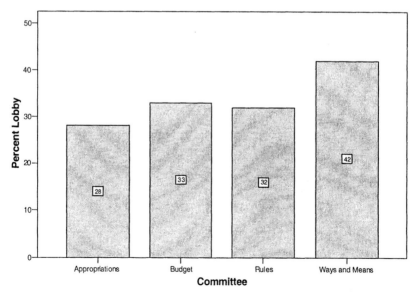

The evidence suggests that a significant portion of former House members-turned lobbyists come from those committees that place members of Congress in a powerful position to reward or punish fellow colleagues, special interest groups, or members of the executive branch. The evidence from the House suggests that specialization in specific policy areas may not necessarily be as valuable as the general policy expertise that may be attributed to members of the prestige committees. While valued, membership in the policy committees is not as valued as having been a member of a powerful prestige committee. As Table 3.3 demonstrated in the earlier chapter, members of the more powerful committees become lobbyists with greater frequency than do those who serve on the more specialized policy and constituency committees like Judiciary and Education and labor.

Former member of Congress, Lee Hamilton raises the question that lawmakers are increasingly not doing the hard work that is required for becoming policy experts. He writes, "Congress is also increasingly punting on one of its key functions: oversight. Performing vigorous and informed oversight is one of the vital functions of the Congress. It demands tedious, technical and often unglamorous work" (Hamilton 2004). Hamilton detects a trend where policy is created in the conference committees as opposed to the standing committees, which is where fact-finding and deliberation occurs. "On three recent far-reaching domestic initiatives - tax cuts, a rewrite of the Medicare rules, and a new energy strategy - the responsibility for crafting legislation was left to conference committees. The regular committees were bypassed," writes Hamilton (2004). When lawmakers fail in their responsibility to become well informed, public policy suffers. The evidence, although a bit tenuous, hints at the possibility that policy expertise is not the primary value of exiting lawmakers. If policy expertise is not what makes an ex-lawmaker valuable to special interests, then something else must be driving the demand for ex-lawmakers to become lobbyists.

Procedural Expertise

A second explanation as to why some lawmakers are more highly prized as lobbyists than others is that they know the legislative process. Knowing how things get done is as important as knowing the policy issues. "Former members have advantages outsiders never have," states Paul Hendrie, with the Center for Responsive Politics. "They know the process inside and out" (Murphy 1999, A1). Richard Shapiro, executive director of the Congressional Management Foundation, similarly focuses on this second type of knowledge when he states:

> The demand for knowledgeable people who can track what is going
> on Capitol Hill and the Government and can figure out the pressure

points that companies should be touching in Washington has greatly increased" (Abramson 1998, A1).

The value in knowing the process is something that former members of Congress stress. Former Congress member Bill Paxon, in a 2003 interview was asked what he had learned about lobbying as a result of being on both sides of the lobby. He responded:

> Although I have to say truthfully being on the Hill, being in public office for 21 years and being lobbied and part of lobbying coalitions when you're trying to move issues, gives you a pretty good insight into most of the things involved (Paxon 2003, 15).

It is the *moving of issues*, rather than the issues themselves that are the focus of the response. Successful lobbyists arrive in Washington knowing the process.

Knowing the legislative process has become far more important to interest groups than in the past because of the changing nature of the legislative process. Hamilton writes, "Longstanding traditions, procedures and values are being pushed aside" (2004). The increased use of omnibus bills to create legislation, coupled with the increased threat to filibuster bills in the Senate, and diffused power in the House has shifted the dynamics of how a bill becomes a law. Barbara Sinclair describes this change in the legislative process in her book, *Unorthodox Lawmaking*. She writes:

> Rather than being sent to one committee in each chamber, many measures are considered by several committees, especially in the House, while some measures bypass committees altogether. Not frequently, after a bill has been reported but before it reaches the floor, major substantive changes are worked out via informal processes. Omnibus measures of great scope are a regular part of the legislative scene and formal executive-congressional summits to work out deals on legislation are no longer considered extraordinary. On the House floor most major measures are considered under complex and unusually restrictive rules, often tailored to deal with problems specific to that bill. In the Senate bills are regularly subject to large numbers of not-necessarily-germane floor amendments; filibuster threats are an every-day fact of life, affecting all aspects of the legislative process and making cloture votes a routine part of the process (1997, 5).

These changes have made policymaking far more complex than policymaking once was. Some are suggesting that the deliberative process is being circumvented by the changes. Congressman Hamilton has written, "Huge supplementals or omnibus bills have made a mockery of legislative process, and important bills have bypassed committees and debate" (Hamilton 2004). In order to be successful as a lobbyist, one would have to be well aware of this shift in policymaking. None would be more aware of this shift in policy making than lawmakers serving in Congress during the end of the 20th Century and beginning of the 21st. Lawmakers serving in Congress during the 1970s and 80s experienced firsthand the new "unorthodox lawmaking" (Sinclair 1997).

Gradually lawmakers began to realize that there was value in knowing the legislative process. Former Representative Jim Slattery who now lobbies for a variety of interests has observed, "Anyone who needs help in Washington is going to want someone who knows Washington," (Murphy 1999, A1). This is an idea that has gained credence among many lobbying firms. The increase in post-congressional lobbying demonstrates that the lobbying firms and special interest groups have gradually become aware of the talents of ex-lawmakers as lobbyists. Some have suggested that some lawmakers are leaving public service earlier than in the past because they want to capitalize on their legislative careers. Thomas Boggs observes:

> [T]here are a lot more former Members who are retiring at midlife. But there are a lot of midlife Members of Congress leaving. Dennis Eckert quit. There are a bunch of guys like that in town who are good young guys that are becoming pretty effective Washington lawyer-lobbyists, what have you. That wasn't as true fifteen years ago (Center for Public Integrity 1997b).

Those who become lobbyists leave office at a younger age – 55 years of age compared to 58 years of age for non-lobbyists. Interestingly, while there are age differences between the lobbyists and non-lobbyists, there are no differences in terms of years of service. Both lobbyists and non-lobbyists have served an average of 15 years before retiring. This suggests that while post-congressional lobbyists leave office at a younger age, they have as much experience as those who leave at a latter age. Post-congressional lobbyists know the process as well as those who do not become lobbyists as measured by the number of years of service.

Friends Lobby Friends

A third explanation is that ex-lawmakers are preferred as lobbyists because they have powerful friends – their former colleagues in Congress and their aides. Former House member Bob Livingston who founded the Livingston Group, a lobbying firm, shortly after leaving office highlights two things that make him valuable to special interest groups. He has said, "If we understand the process and can get through the front door, that's primarily the reason why clients hire me" (Eilperin 2003, A01). Former lawmakers have many advantages over non-former members of Congress who lobby. They have access to many of the facilities that lawmakers have, including the floor of their respective chambers, free parking in the congressional parking lot, and they do not have to wait in long lines to get into the Capitol to see their former colleagues (Eilperin 2003, A01). Members of Congress work side-by-side for many years. They develop strong relationships with their colleagues and become good friends. They trust each other's counsel, and as a consequence develop the type of relationship that can later blur the line between friend and lobbyist. Former members of Congress have access to their former colleagues and this makes them valuable. The perception among special interest groups is that ex-lawmakers have the connections that they need. Walker Merryman, a Vice President with the Tobacco Institute justified the hiring of Robin Tallon a former Congress member from South Carolina because he has familiarity with his former colleagues. He states, "Simply by the fact that he [Representative Tallon] knows these people and they know him, yes, he would have greater access" (Jakubiak 2004). But it is not just a perception among special interest groups that ex-lawmakers have access. Repeatedly ex-lawmakers who have become lobbyists point out that what makes them valuable as lobbyists is that they are able to gain access to lawmakers. Former Congressman, Guy Vader Jagt makes this point clear when he says, "The fact that I served with [members] on the conference committees on the tax bills over the years and we've been through the fire together made them probably more likely to see me than someone who had not shared that experience" (Marcus, 1997 A01). "Access, I suppose, always helps outcomes," said Congressman Barney Frank who helped write the law that banned former members of Congress from lobbying for one year (Eilperin 2003). Some exiting lawmakers shun the idea of providing access. Exiting Lawmaker Don Nickles said, "I don't see myself on Capitol Hill knocking on doors" (Birnbaum 2004, A01). But access is only half the battle. The other half deals with getting the legislators to do what the lobbyists want them to do. Kenneth J. Kies who lobbies for Price Waterhouse Coopers and once served under House Ways and Means Chairman Bill Archer says of members of Congress, "They don't do things because someone who's a buddy of theirs comes to see them" (Abramson 1998). Former Archer aid and Whitehouse Press Secretary Ari Flisher further notes, "There are scores of top-notch lobbyists who have relationships but who don't have the great knowledge to go beyond a handshake" (Abramson 1998, A1). Access and information is what makes these former lawmakers valuable lobbyists.

A particular type of friend is the partisan friend. After the Republican Party won control of Congress in 1994, Republican lawmakers pressured firms to hire more lobbyists. Majority Whip Tom Delay in 1995 as well as House Financial Services Committee Chairman Michael Oxley's staff have been criticized for having instructed those hoping to do business with the Republican controlled Congress to hire more Republicans (Maraniss, Weisskopf 1995 A1 and VandeHei and Day 2003 A4). "There are an awful lot of [lobbying] firms looking around and saying, 'Hey, we have no Republicans,'" says former Majority Leader Dick Armey who worked for the lobbying firm Piper Rudnick upon retiring from Congress. "All of a sudden, after four years, this is a Republican town, not a Democratic town" (Russell Chaddock, 2003). "Ninety percent of the new top hires are going to Republicans; it should be 100 percent," says Grover Norquist. As a consequence of this increased demand for Republican lobbyists, many former Republican lawmakers moved into lobbying careers. Since the 104th Congress 59 percent of all ex-lawmakers-turned-lobbyists are Republicans and 41 percent are Democrats.

Lawmakers are afforded access for another reason as well. Given the low pay that congressional staff receive, it is not uncommon for these aides to move around, developing expertise in one policy area and then moving into a government agency or an interest group. When lawmakers leave office to become lobbyists, some will have a small army of former staff members willing to receive them either as partners with prestigious lobbying firms or as lobbyists attempting to influence a government agency. "You can almost not find an agency in this government that does not have an Armey guy in it," boasts former Majority Leader Dick Armey (Russell Chaddock, 2003). With so many staff people moving in and out of offices, lawmakers with connections to these staff people have great access to policy makers and as a consequence are highly prized as lobbyists.

Post-Congressional Lobbyists And Legislation

Thus far it has been suggested that post-congressional lobbyists behave differently from non-lobbying ex-lawmakers. The notion that post-congressional lobbyists are wanted as lobbyists because they know policy has also been partially dismissed. Perhaps a better explanation is that ex-lawmakers are wanted for their procedural knowledge. It is also suggested that post-congressional lobbyists are wanted because their former colleagues are also their friends. Now we test a more rigorous model of legislative activity. Here, as in earlier models (Santos 2003, and Santos 2004) I test the effect of post-congressional lobbying on legislative activity. I will identify variables that are correlated with the number of bills that exiting lawmakers sponsor during their last term. Essentially I want to show the relationship between the number of bills sponsored by a retiring lawmaker and the lawmaker's post-congressional career choice. It is assumed that lawmakers who are leaving office will become less active because they no longer worry about being removed from office. I hypothesize that among those who eventually become lobbyists, there is less of an inclination to decrease their legislative activity. Those who become lobbyists continue to sponsor legislation that benefits their future employers. I test the following the following hypotheses:

- Ex-lawmakers who become lobbyists will remain more active during their last term than their non-lobbying colleagues.
- Senators will be more active during their last term than House members.
- Republicans will be less active than Democrats because Republicans prefer a smaller government.
- Younger lawmakers will be more active than older lawmakers.
- Lawmakers with a longer tenure will be less active than lawmakers with a shorter tenure.
- High-ranking committee members will be less active than low-ranking committee members.
- Legislators who were active during their penultimate term will be active during their last term.

These are the various hypotheses that will be tested. Very briefly I will explain the logic behind each of these hypotheses. Regarding the first hypothesis, it is assumed that ex-lawmakers who will become lobbyists remain active not for the sake of impressing their constituents but for the sake of impressing their future employers. Lawmakers may want to demonstrate vitality, understanding, or perhaps to show sympathy for a particular position. One way of doing these things is to submit bills. Even if the goal is not to create legislation, it gives the soon to be unemployed lawmaker a few more lines on his resume. It is important to introduce a few bills just so that representatives can at least claim to have tried to do something about some particular issue. Senators are also expected to be more active than House members during their last term. Senators will be more active than their House colleagues simply because there are fewer Senators than there are House members introducing a sizeable number of bills. In the 107th Congress, each House member introduced about 13 bills on average. In the Senate, each Senator introduced about 31 bills – more than two bills for every House bill introduced. In the model to be presented shortly, party is also controlled for. It is assumed that Republicans, being against big government will be less active during their last term than Democrats. While this may be a stereotype more so than actual reality, it nevertheless is worth controlling for. Lawmakers who are older or having served a longer tenure when they leave office will be less active during their last term. The assumption here is that those who are too old are leaving office so that they may slow down the pace of life. Those who have served lengthy terms are expected to be less active for a different reason. Those with longer tenures are more successful at enacting legislation. As a consequence they are less likely to engage in frivolous bill sponsorship. The same reasoning applies for lawmakers who rank high in the various standing committees. The model will also control for the number of bills sponsored during the penultimate term. Those lawmakers who have been active in the past are expected to be active during the last term as well. Lastly, I will control for the effect of the circumstances under which the lawmaker left office.

Those who left voluntarily and thus would have been in a position to plan their retirement are expected to remain active, while those who were defeated at reelection or who ran for a higher office are expected not to have changed much. The model will be tested using a multivariate regression equation. It will show the relationship between the number of bills sponsored by members of Congress during their last term (legislative activity) and the variables identified in the hypotheses above.

I have identified 798 former members of Congress[2]. Of these, 659 are former members of the House and 139 are former Senators. Two hundred forty-one, or 30 percent have been registered as lobbyists since leaving office. Lobbyists were identified using a number of editions of the *Directory of Registered Lobbyists*. Democrats account for a greater percentage of retirees – accounting for 59 percent. Republicans have made up 41 percent of the ex-lawmakers. Of the 798 former lawmakers included in this study, 32 percent were defeated for reelection, 49 percent left voluntarily, and 19 percent sought a different office. These lawmakers served an average of fifteen years in Congress, and retired, on average, at the age of 57. The one variable that needs a little explaining is the *committee rank*. Committee rank is a measure of the average rank on the different committees that the lawmaker served on. So, if a lawmaker served on two committees, and was ranked third in one and fourth in the second, the average score would be 3.5. The lower the number the more senior the lawmaker[3].

Table 4.1 shows the results from the regression equation. The model shows that all of the variables except *age* and *political party* are correlated to the number of bills introduced during the last term. Perhaps understandably so, the biggest predictor of legislative activity during a lawmaker's last term in office is the legislative activity of lawmakers during the second to the last Congress before leaving office. Those who have a history of being active tended to remain so, while those who tended to be less active tended to remain less active during the last term. Those lawmakers who have served long tenures at the time that they left Congress tended to be less active than those with shorter tenures. This is so even after controlling for *age*, which has no direct relationship on bill sponsorship during the last term in office. As hypothesized, members of the Senate tend to be more active than their colleagues in the House. The average rank on congressional committees is also significantly correlated with bill sponsorship. Those lawmakers who are more highly ranked tend to be more active during their last term.

Table 4.1: Explaining Bill Sponsorship During the Last Term in Office.

Variable	B Coefficients (Standard Error)
Post-Congressional Lobbyist	2.10*
	(1.065)
Bill Sponsorship During Penultimate	.582***
Term	(.021)
Age	.083
	(.060)
Tenure	-.286***
	(.078)
Chamber	7.577***
	(1.35)
Committee Rank	-2.17*
	(.106)
Party	.274
	(1.1)
Constant	-1.278
	(4.343)
R2	.56

Significance
* .05
** .01
*** .0001

Of primary importance for this book is the first variable in table 4.1. *Post-Congressional Lobbyist*, the variable measuring whether the lawmaker is a lobbyist or not is significantly correlated with legislative activity. The coefficient is 2.1 and is significant at the .05 level.[4] Controlling for other factors, the table indicates that the number of bills introduced during the last term are higher among those who eventually become lobbyists and decrease among those who do not become lobbyists. Ex-lawmakers who become lobbyists upon leaving office remain active during their last term in office. They are much more likely to sponsor bills than their non-lobbying colleagues. This might suggest a couple things. One of these things is that these lawmakers know they are leaving and so they are sending signals to prospective clients. There is some evidence to support this notion. In an earlier test of a similar model I found that post-congressional lobbyists who left voluntarily, and thus could plan for their exit, remained more active than those who were ousted from their seats, or who sought a higher office (Santos 2004).

Thus far I have measured legislative activity as being bill sponsorship. Clearly there is limited harm in sponsoring bills if the goal is to send signals to prospective employers. The only ethical breach may come if "job negotiations are underway" (The Committee on Standards of Official Conduct 1992). While at no point do I find retiring lawmakers explicitly negotiating jobs for policy, at this point the focus will be on the success that ex-lawmakers have at ensuring that their bills become laws. Thus far it has been shown that lawmakers who become lobbyists tend to behave differently during their last term in office than their colleagues who do not become lobbyists. It has been shown that they remain active during their last term in office, primarily sponsoring legislation. What about legislative success, i.e. success in getting bills turned into actual laws? Under limited conditions, lawmakers who become lobbyists upon leaving office also tend to be more successful in insuring that their bills become laws.

Among House members who retire voluntarily, I find a significant relationship between the number of laws sponsored by the exiting lawmaker and whether the lawmaker becomes a lobbyist or not, upon leaving office. As before, I test a multivariate model. But while the dependent variable in the earlier model was the number of bills sponsored, in this model the dependent variable is the number of *laws* that the lawmaker sponsored during the last term in office. Unlike before, this model only looks at members of the House of Representatives who left office *voluntarily*. As stated previously, it is those who left voluntarily who are best positioned to become lobbyists. They can take advantage of the next two years to insure that certain bills become laws. There are a total of 317 lawmakers who served in the House and left the House Voluntarily. Of these, 28 percent have become lobbyists. I also look at similar variables as in the earlier model, except that I have excluded the members' party affiliation and members of the Senate.[5] As before, I control for the number of laws sponsored by the lawmaker during the penultimate legislative session, the average rank on the various committees, age and tenure. I also control for a new variable – one that controls for whether the retiring lawmaker was a member of the majority or minority party at the time of departure from Congress. I include this variable because it is expected that lawmakers who are in the minority party will be less successful in enacting legislation.

Table 4.2 shows the results from the equation. The model shows that a significant portion of the variance in the number of public laws sponsored by the House members who are voluntarily retiring can be explained by the variables in the equation. I should note that *age* is not detected as significant at the .05 level, but was significant at .055. So, while it is not significant by the conventional measure, it comes close to being significant. I find that tenure and average committee rank are significantly related to the number of laws sponsored by the lawmakers. These relationships are negative, suggesting that the more seasoned lawmakers are the sponsors of fewer laws than their less seasoned colleagues. I also find that being in the majority party contributes to legislative success. Those who are in the majority will be the sponsors of more laws than those who are in the minority party. As before, I controlled for the number of laws that the exiting lawmaker sponsored during the penultimate session, and found a strong relationship.

Table 4.2: Explaining House Legislative Success During the Last Term in Office.

Variable	B Coefficients (Standard Error)
Post-Congressional Lobbyist	.35*
	(.175)
Laws Sponsored During	.541***
Penultimate Term	(.039)
Age	.019
	(.010)
Tenure	-.045***
	(.012)
Majority/Minority Status	.64***
	(.167)
Committee Rank	-.042**
	(.016)
Constant	-.228
	(.578)
R2	.474

Significance
* .05
**.01
*** .0001

Having controlled for these variables we can now turn to the more important of the variables – the post-congressional lobbying variable. The data shows a significant correlation between the number of laws sponsored by the exiting lawmakers, and whether they become lobbyists or not. Those lawmakers who become lobbyists are significantly more legislatively successful than their non-lobbying counterparts. Those who become lobbyists are the sponsors of more laws than those who do not become lobbyists. This evidence suggests that lawmakers who become lobbyists and who are in a position to plan their exit from the House of Representatives, also take advantage of that time to ensure that more of their bills become laws – this in comparison to their non-lobbying counterparts. With legislative success, it looks less and less like post-congressional lobbyists are simply sending signals to prospective employers. Lawmakers may be rewarding their future employers. To address this possibility in greater detail one would have to connect the laws that were sponsored by the post-congressional lobbyists to the interest groups that they represent. And even once that has been shown, the intentional rewarding of future employers has not been definitively and unequivocally shown. It could be argued that post-congressional lobbyists become lobbyists because they are successful at ensuring that their bills become laws. That is to say, they are wanted as lobbyists because they are successful in enacting legislation, rather than that they are successful at enacting legislation because they hope to become lobbyists. The next chapter will address this possibility. For now it is worth describing some additional observations that show an anecdotal but interesting connection between the laws sponsored and the interest groups that the lawmakers go to work for.

The interests that lawmakers lobby for tend to have several connections to the lawmakers. In many instances the special interest groups have a state or regional focus. For instance an ex-lawmaker from Houston who becomes a lobbyist may lobby for the energy sector, or a lawmaker from Michigan may lobby on behalf of the auto industry. A second connection is that post-congressional lobbyists lobby for groups with issues pending before the lawmakers' committees or recently resolved by the lawmakers' committees. The majority of lawmakers who become lobbyists actually lobby on behalf of interests that would have been served by the lawmakers' committee. Many Congress members, like Lloyd Meeds from Washington State, who served on the Natural Resources Committee, will become lobbyists for interests regulated by the committee on which they once served. Congressman Meeds' own clients included fishing, mining, and hazardous material transporting interests. Some of the most blatant connections between the legislative activity of the post-congressional lobbyists and the groups on whose behalf they lobby manifest themselves.

During the 108th Congress, Congressman Billy Tauzin, the Chair of the Energy and Commerce Committee announced his retirement from the House. It was Congressman Tauzin and the Energy and Commerce Committee that played a central role in ensuring the enactment of the Medicare Prescription Drug, Improvement, and Modernization Act of 2003. During the late 1990s and early 2000, state governments began to experiment with policies that would reduce the cost of Medicare and the soaring cost of prescription drugs. The State of Maine was one of the first states to regulate prices. Maine Rx, as the law would come to be known, gave the state of Maine the power to negotiate with pharmaceutical companies for better drug prices. Because the state could use Medicare and Medicaid as a bargaining chip with the pharmaceutical companies, Maine was in a position to dictate prices to the pharmaceutical companies wishing to preserve a slice of the Medicare and Medicaid budget. Such bargaining power frightened the industry. Marjorie Powell, Senior Assistant General Counsel for Pharmaceutical Research and Manufacturers of America (PhRMA), appearing on *Frontline* (a PBS television program) would respond, "We don't think the government should be setting prices and telling companies what they can charge. We think that prices should be set through the market, through negotiations. That's the way the private sector works" (2003). The pharmaceutical industry quickly sued the state, winning an injunction on the new law, but on March 5th of 2001, the First Circuit Court of Appeals in Boston agreed with Maine and lifted the injunction. PhRMA then took a two-pronged approach. It appealed the case to the Supreme Court and also began to lobby Congress for its own version of drug coverage for seniors. Marjorie Powell would defend PhRMA's new position saying, "In this day and age, when drugs are such an important part of the healthcare system to have the federal program for seniors not cover drugs just makes no sense. So we're urging members of Congress to enact a Medicare drugs benefit" (2003). This was the time for the pharmaceutical industry to turn to Congress. On January 22, 2003 the US Supreme Court heard the Maine Rx case and upheld the state of Maine's law. Richard Evans, a Senior Research Analyst with Global Pharmaceuticals at Sanford C. Bernstein and Company describes the industry's decision to lobby Congress:

> The drug industry views a Medicare drug benefit as ultimately inevitable. If that is your conviction, then you want to have that drug benefit passed on the best possible terms. And I think the industry feels that with a Republican in the White House and Republican majorities in both chambers of Congress, that now's the time (2003).

Enter Billy Tauzin and the Energy and Commerce Committee. He was one of a handful of members of Congress to be singled out by the President for his efforts on the Medicare Prescription Drug, Improvement and Modernization Act of 2003, when he signed the bill into law (Bush, 2003). The committee played a central role in ensuring that the federal government would not be able to dictate drug prices to the pharmaceutical companies.

The President of the United States signed the law on December 8, 2003. By February of 2004, less than three months later, the news was out that Chairman Tauzin was entertaining the notion of becoming a lobbyist for PhRMA, the lobbying arm of the pharmaceutical industry. The media quickly pointed out that it was unseemly of the chairman who had been central to the redesigning of the Medicare laws so as to benefit the pharmaceutical industry to be contemplating a career move from congressman to lobbyist for the pharmaceutical industry (Alpert and Walsh 2004, 9). Under pressure, he quickly withdrew his name from consideration.

His name has been tossed around for a number of lobbing positions. He has been considered a possible replacement for Jack Valenti, the lobbyist for the movie industry, and he has even "auditioned" for the position of lobbyist for the Recording Industry Association. He and Congresswoman Mary Bono sang a Rap song at the going-away party for Hilary Rosen, the lobbyist for the Recording Industry Association. By video, Congressman Tauzin reported, "We know the house rules don't allow us to apply for the job, but there is nothing wrong with auditioning for it. " The song, sung by Mary Bono and Billy Tauzin continues:

Mary: I'm ready.
Both: Who wants the job of Hilary Rosen?

> How 'bout the dream team of Bono and Tauzin.
> **Billy**:   We heard the rumors going around town.
> **Mary**: That Mary and Billy could take Kazaa down.
> **Billy**:   We know your problems inside and out.
> **Mary**: Burnin' CD's...Ooooh...A very scary thought
> **Billy:**   Piracy bad.
> **Both**:   Piracy bad. Piracy bad. Piracy bad.
> **Billy:**   For a million a year. We'll tell them punks...
> **Mary**: Steal our songs, we'll break rock into chunks
> **Billy:**   I love music, how 'bout 'Sonny and Cher'
> **Mary**: I love royalties, so kids please be fair.
> **Billy:**   You still don't think we're the ones for the job?
> Yo we're politicians. We were born to hob-knob
> **Both**:   Piracy bad. Piracy bad. Piracy bad (Grove 2003, C03).

This skit, while comical, demonstrates the increasingly brazen behavior of members of Congress, when it comes to pursuing post-congressional lobbying careers. The popular press is beginning to speculate that lawmakers secretly envy lobbyists. Timothy Noah with Slate Magazine writes:

> Just a generation ago, the only two reasons even a low-ranking member might leave the House of Representatives were if he lost an election or if he retired. It was not a foregone conclusion that he would stay in Washington, but if he did, and he took a lobbying job, the appropriate feeling to have toward him was mild pity. Sure, he'd be paid more. But the best years of his life would be behind him. Inside his comfortable office, he'd gaze out the window and daydream about his glory days in government.

> Today, it's different. House members actually leave Congress *voluntarily*, sometimes before serving out their terms, to become lobbyists. It isn't cause to feel sorry for them. It's usually just assumed they will stay in Washington, and as lobbyists, they will stand at the top of the heap. Today, members of Congress gaze out their windows and daydream about becoming lobbyists (Noah 2003).

And there is an allure to the profession of lobbyists now that was not there a short time ago. For an ex-lawmaker, lobbying results in less work, for more money. And increasingly, ones fellow lobbyists are come from the ranks of former speakers of the House, majority and minority leaders, and high-ranking members of the executive branch. The attractiveness of the position has changed, and now more than ever, being a lawmaker is no longer an end in itself. Increasingly public service has become a means to an end – the end being joining the lobbying profession.

[1] The history I reference is the legislators' legislative activity during their penultimate session.

[2] The data identifying those members who became lobbyists during the period 1984 through 1996 comes from the Rebecca Borders and C.C. Dockery's text Beyond the Hill: A Directory of Congress from 1984 to 1993 Where Have All the Members Gone? (Lanham MD: University Press of America, 1995); Arthur C. Close, and John P. Gregg, eds. Washington Representatives, (Washington D.C.: Columbia Books Inc., 1987); Arthur C. Close, Gregory L. Bologna and John P. Gregg, eds. Washington Representatives, (Washington D.C.: Columbia Books Inc., Publishers 1989);   M.A. Bettelheim, Directory of Registered Federal Lobbyists. 1st ed. (Orange, NJ: Academic Media, 1973); and The Center For responsive Politics accessed June 4, 2002 http://www.crp.org/lobbyists/database.htm. Additional data identifying ex-lawmakers comes from ICPSR data set 7803 Inter-university Consortium for Political and Social Research and Carroll McKibbin. "Roster of United States Congressional Officeholders and Biographical Characteristics of Members of the United States Congress, 1789-1996: Merged Data [Computer file]. 10th ICPSR ed. Ann Arbor, MI: Inter-university Consortium for Political and Social Research [producer and distributor], 1997.

[3] Given that some lawmakers serve on more than one committee it was necessary to take into account all of these committees. But, to ensure one rank score as opposed to as many rank scores as there are committees that a lawmaker may served, I felt an average of these scores was in order.

[4] The measure for the variable Post-Congressional Lobbyist is coded 0 and 1 – 0 if the lawmaker did not become a lobbyist, and 1 if the lawmaker did become a lobbyist.

[5] I tried the model including these variables but found that they were significantly correlated with the dependent variable.

5

Public Policy and the Interest Group Connection: Five Case Studies

Those who lobby can be categorized into different types of lobbyists. Some can are *state lobbyists*. These are former lawmakers who lobby on behalf of state interests. State lobbyists will lobby for state and local governments from their own states, or they may lobby for corporations found within the state that they represented at one point. These lobbyists tend to capitalize on their connections to former campaign contributors. Being that lawmakers raise a significant amount of money from special interests from within their own state, many post-congressional lobbyists will have developed strong relationships with these former campaign contributors. A different type of lobbyist is the *industry lobbyist*. Industry lobbyists are those post-congressional lobbyists who lobby either strictly or almost strictly for one industry. Many of these *industry lobbyists* are former lawmakers who served on congressional committees with some oversight over the industry on whose behalf they would lobby upon leaving office. Post-congressional lobbyists can also be categorized as being the lobbyists of *major* and *minor clients*. Major clients come from those industries with very deep pockets and that are able to raise a significant amount of money for candidates. They come from highly organized industries that have been under public pressure to take some action that they would rather avoid. It is often times under public pressure that major clients become major clients. They make significant contributions and hire the most powerful lobbyists, including former lawmakers when they are under pressure to take action that they otherwise would not like to take. An example here might be the rise of the tobacco industry in the 1990s. Prior to the 1990s, when there were no major threats of weakening or destroying the industry, the tobacco lobbyists were not as active as they would become in the mid 1990s. The lobbyists of minor clients, by contrast tend to be ignored by the general public. Their interests are not particularly important to the general public, and as a consequence, are able to obtain concessions with some success. The dredging industry, which helps to clear waterways, is of this type. Generally, it does not receive a lot of attention from the press, and so lobbyists for companies in these industries are able to gain significant concessions by being inconspicuous. Many post-congressional lobbyists are some combination of these categories. It is not uncommon for a post-congressional lobbyist to represent state interests and part of some industry that has no connection to the post-congressional lobbyist's former district or state.

Post-congressional lobbyists who are successful at enacting legislation are most successful with legislation that provides funding for pork-barrel projects. Most enactments deal with land transfers, funding for infrastructure projects, and public buildings. Banking, trade, appropriations and taxes account for a quarter of the laws sponsored by retiring lawmakers.[1] Showing the connection between the laws sponsored by post-congressional lobbyists and the special interest groups that they go to work for upon leaving office is not an easy task. Often times, the connections are tucked away in omnibus legislation. Sometimes, it is a subtle change in policy – changing a minor section of an existing law. At other times, the connection is based on what is not enacted as in the case of the Medicare reform proposal discussed in the earlier chapter. Given the difficulty in showing the connections, one must rely on the case study method to test for the connection between the policy and the interest group on whose behalf the lawmaker lobbies. This chapter will present the case of five ex-lawmakers who would become lobbyists upon leaving office. It will show the connection between public policy and the groups on whose behalf the ex-lawmakers would lobby. The first of these case studies will focus on charter schools and Congressman Frank Riggs, a California congressman who, before leaving office, helped to increase funding for charter schools only to retire from Congress to go work for the Charter School Development Corporation. Then there is the story of Congressman John Myers and others, who helped revitalize the dredging industry while in office and then later while out of office. This story will be followed by the case of the Rural Electric Cooperative and the role that Congressman Glenn English played in its salvation. I follow the story of the Rural Electric Cooperative with the case of the National Rife Association, the Firearms Owners' Protection Act, and Congressman Harold Volkmer. Lastly, there is the case of Senator Wendell Ford, who fought to protect tobacco interests while in Congress, and later would lobby on the behalf of tobacco interests while out of the Senate. These cases will show the connection between the issues that members of Congress promoted while in Congress, and the special interest groups that they would work for upon leaving their respective chambers.

Charter Schools, the Charter School Development Corporation and Frank Riggs

The charter school movement has been one of the most significant attempts at systematically reforming public education in the United States. The first charter schools were implemented by the School District of Philadelphia, a district with a history of trying new and innovative educational programs (Schwartz 1994, 111). By the early 1990s Minnesota and California had also begun similar efforts. In 2003, forty states, Puerto Rico and the District of Columbia had joined in on the new educational reform effort (US Charter Schools 2004). The goal was to provide educational opportunities to parents. The expectation was that parents, dissatisfied with the performance of their children's schools would enroll their students in charter schools – smaller, less bureaucratic schools that typically received their authority from the state rather than the public school district. One hope was that increased competition for students would force large school districts to become more efficient and effective for fear of losing funding tied to student enrollment.

Charter schools differ from public schools in many ways. They tend to be smaller, they tend to serve minority populations at a higher rate than whites, and they tend to serve poor populations at a higher rate than public schools (U.S. Department of Education 2000). They also tend be more autonomous, and financially strapped (U.S. Department of Education 2000). In a study conducted by the US Department of Education, respondents reported that "Realizing an alternative vision for schooling was the most important reason for founding charter schools" (U.S. Department of Education 2000). In fact, many charter schools have developed niche programs for specific interests. Developing highly specialized programs that often times break from the methods of school districts is one of the appeals of charter schools.

The growth in the number of charter schools exploded in the United States with the passage of the Charter School Expansion Act of 1998, Public Law 105-278. By 2004 some 3,000 charter schools were in operation (Center for Education Reform 2004). The number of new schools has increased exponentially. Figure 5.1 shows the number of new charter schools that were begun between the years 1993 through 2003. In less than ten years, the number of charter schools had increased on 2000 to a high of 623 new charter schools. These schools instruct over half a million students in the United States (National Education Association 2002). And that number is growing with the addition of each new charter school, although the numbers have slowed somewhat. Since 2000 the number of new charter schools has decreased to about 300 per year (see Figure 5.1).

Figure 5.1: Estimated Number of New Charter Schools Opening by School Year

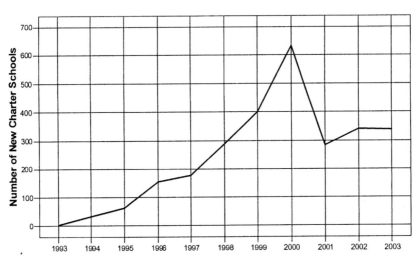

Source: 1993-1999 US Department of Education http://www.ed.gov/pubs/charter4thyear/index.html. 2000-2002 data from Stateline.org. 2003 data comes from the Center for Educational Reformhttp://www.edreform.com/index.cfm?fuseAction=document&documentID=1760&sectionID=34&NEWSYEAR=2004.

This decrease has come under a torrent of bad press. Critics have pointed to the mismanagement of these schools, the poor student performance, ill-equipped instructors, dilapidated facilities, and the use of public money to fund religious education as some of the problems with charter schools (National Education Association 2002). Some of these problems were becoming evident even in 1998, the year Congress increased spending for charter schools (Poole 1998, 24, Rothstein 1998, 46). Perhaps most alarming is that there were few efforts to evaluate student performance at these schools (Rothstein 1998, 46). The US Department of Education's focus on student assessment was limited to a discussion on the number of assessment tools used in the various states (U.S. Department of Education 2000). With relatively little data, the federal government embarked on a hundred million dollar expansion of charter schools (Section 3.i, Public Law 105-278).[2] The sparse data on the performance of charter schools was something that even the sponsor of the Charter School Expansion Act recognized, stating, "Early reports, and I stress that they are very preliminary, early reports indicate parental satisfaction"... (Riggs, 1997a, 6) The five hearings held by the Subcommittee on Early Childhood, Youth and Families and the Oversight Subcommittee found anecdotal data showing support for charter schools. Congressman Frank Riggs chaired the congressional subcommittee Early Childhood, Youth and Families of the House Education and

Workforce Committee. On October 9, 1997, Riggs' opening remarks summarized the evidence:

> At these hearings, parents, students, charter schoolteachers, and administrators testified that charter schools are working, and more importantly, charter schools are making many positive contributions to the quality of public education. We heard over and over about small teacher-student ratios, how parents were welcome at the schools at any time, how teachers were free to be innovative, and how administrators were set-free from unnecessary paper work (Riggs 1997b).

This data primarily showed levels of satisfaction with the autonomy provided by charter schools, but little evidence showing student performance was reported. When the problems with charter schools were discussed, the primary concern was with accessing federal funding. Congressman Riggs reported the findings of a General Accounting Office report, which suggested that state enrollment rules, along with monetary and time costs associated with applying for funding were the primary constraints facing charter schools (Riggs 1997). In 1997, there is less concern with student success than with funding and expanding charter schools.

About the same time that the Charter School Expansion Act was being debated in Congress, a new non-profit organization was formed in Washington DC. In June of 1997, the Charter Schools Development Corporation (CSDC) was incorporated.[3] Its mission is to provide financial and technical assistance to charter schools. "CSDC is dedicated to helping charter schools solve their facility needs, using the District of Columbia as a model for public-private partnerships that can be readily replicated and expanded nationwide" (Charter School Development Corporation 2002). The CSDC website boasts of the organization's legislative success, "Nationally, CSDC initiated a legislative effort that resulted in Congress authorizing $100 million, and appropriating $25 million, for a facilities financing demonstration program" (Charter School Development Corporation 2002). These 100 million dollars is the same amount that was appropriated by Congress under the Charter School Expansion Act of 1998, which was sponsored by Congressman Frank Riggs. Riggs was able to lead the bill through Congress insuring its passage.

Shortly after the passage of the Charter School Expansion Act, Congressman Frank Riggs retired from Congress. He joined the Heritage Foundation as a Visiting Scholar in early 1999. The president of the Heritage Foundation, Edwin Feulner, would say of Riggs, "No member of Congress has been more involved with education matters, or better understands the need for education reform" (Sack and McQueen 1998, 23). The Heritage Foundation has been a strong supporter of charter schools and voucher programs.

The same year that Frank Riggs began his post as a visiting scholar, Cathy and Frank Riggs founded Riggs Government Relations Consulting. On July 1, 1999, Cathy and Frank Riggs filed lobbying disclosure forms. Riggs Government Relations Consulting would sign up as one of its first clients the Charter Schools Development Corporation (CSDC). This firm was incorporated the same year that the Charter School Expansion Act was being debated in Congress. In their lobbying report, Riggs Government Relations Consulting reports a lobbying income for representing the Charter Schools Development Corporation of 20,000 dollars. The firm would also begin to lobby for Edupoint, a firm that develops software for the management of school districts (Edupoint.com 2004). In 2000, Riggs would lobby for Edupoint for 15,000 dollars. Both CSDC and Edupoint would have clear interests pending before the House Education and Workforce Committee, Congressman Riggs' former committee, and now, as a lobbyist he would be in a strong position to lobby on their behalf. For a little less than a year and a half, Frank Riggs also served as the Executive Vice President and Chief Operating Officer for CSDC (Charter Schools Development Corporation 2002). Records indicate that by 2001, Riggs was no longer lobbying for either CSDC or Edupoint, but instead was working for Children First/CEO America and Edison Schools Incorporated, making 40,000 and 60,000 dollars from each group respectively (United States Senate Office of Public Records 2004). At this point he also appears as being a lobbyist for Van Scoyoc Associates representing both Children First and Edison. By 2003 he would appear as Vice President of Government Relations and Business Development with Sylvan Education Solutions.

Charter schools continue to grow, although at a slower pace than before. They continue to struggle to make significant improvements in the performance of students. Many of these schools continue to exist in some of the most dilapidated buildings, where ill prepared and ill-equipped teachers assist students. Charter schools have become the place where the students with the greatest need are sent. Even public schools, which were supposed to see charter schools as competition, are incorporating their function into public education. Charter schools are seen as a way of alleviating overcrowding in public schools. They are also being viewed as a way of dealing with disruptive students. Charter schools were to encourage experimentation with fewer resources, and instead a new special interest has been created. Like other special interests, charter schools are organizing, and one of their first demands is increased funding. The hope that competition can be created in public education has stalled. While there are a few glimmers of hope, in the charter school debate, there is much lacking in these schools.

Dredging up the Past

The Great Lakes Dredge and Dock Company (GLDD) is one of the world's largest dredging companies with a history spanning over 100 years (Dredging News Online 2004). William A. Lydon and Fred C. Drews founded the company in 1890 with the construction project of a two-mile long tunnel under Lake Michigan (Great Lakes Dredge and Dock 2004, History). With their success of the first major project, others would soon follow. By the early 1900s, the company had expanded its fleet and began projects outside of the Great Lakes region. Although quite successful, the post-World War II era brought with it a couple of significant changes in attitude that would benefit the Great Lakes Dredge and Dock Company. One of these changes was the federal government's reduction of the Army Corps of Engineers' dredging fleet. Thanks in part to the efforts of John A. Downs, who was the Chairman of the Board of Great Lakes Dredge and Dock Company; the federal government reduced the size of the Corps' dredging fleet (Great Lakes Dredge and Dock 2004, History). According to documents filed with the Securities and Exchange Commission, the Army Corp of Engineers is withdrawing the use of its hopper dredges (Great Lakes Dredge and Dock Corporation: Annual Report Pursuant to Section 13 and 15(d) of the Securities and Exchange Commission 2000, 2). The reduction in the Corps' fleet would increase the role of the private sector in the dredging of waterways (Great Lakes Dredge and Dock Corporation: Annual Report Pursuant to Section 13 and 15(d) of the Securities and Exchange Commission 2000, 2).

The 1980s brought with it further opportunities for the company, when Congress passed the Water Resources Development Act of 1986 (WRDA), also known as the *Deep Ports* legislation (Great Lakes Dredge and Dock 2004, History). The Water Resources Development Act of 1986 called for the construction of "deep-draft harbor projects in Alabama, Mississippi, Louisiana, Texas, Virginia, California, New York and New Jersey (Public Law 99-662). The law called for the construction of numerous "cargo and shallow harbor projects" (Public Law 99-662). "Much of which work was performed by the company," reports the Great Lakes Dredge and Dock Company (Great Lakes Dredge and Dock 2004, History). In all, WRDA called for deepening thirty-nine ports (Great Lakes Dredge and Dock Corporation: Annual Report Pursuant to Section 13 and 15(d) of the Securities and Exchange Commission 2000, 2). This would mean a significant improvement in the value of the company. Figure 5.2 shows the gross profits for the company between 1995 and 2003.[4] The figure shows a dramatic increase in business activity beginning in 1998, and continuing into the present.

Figure 5.2: Great Lakes Dredge and Dock Gross Profit from 1995 to 2003

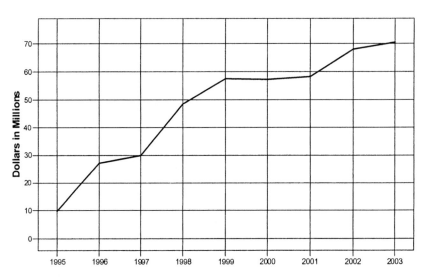

Source: Annual Reports to SEC

The Great Lakes Dredge and Dock Company reported improvements in its business:

> In mid-1996, the domestic dredging market began to improve due to increased demand for dredging capacity for beach nourishment projects and funding for deferred maintenance of harbors and waterways. This trend continued in 1997 with the release by the Corps of maintenance dredging projects for New York and New Jersey that had been on hold pending decisions on disposal of dredged materials. The company won contracts for construction of Pier 400 in Los Angeles, deepening work in Boston Harbor, and bid successfully on Deep Port work in San Juan, Puerto Rico (Great Lakes Dredge and Dock 2004, History).

Part of the reason for the improved market was increased support from Congress. Figure 5.3 shows the percent of contract revenue that was earned by the Great Lakes Dredge and Dock Corporation from contracts with the federal government. The figure shows that since the mid 1990s GLDD has experienced a significant increase in federal contracting revenue. It was about this time that the dredging industry received support from Congress. Retiring Congressman John Meyers sponsored the Energy and Water Development Appropriations Act of 1996, which provided millions of dollars for dredging projects while at the same time further constraining the Army Corps of Engineers from conducting further dredging when the private sector can perform the work at a price not to exceed 25 percent of what the Secretary of the Army deems a fair price (Public Law 104-46 Section 101.b).

Figure 5.3: Percent of Great Lakes Dredge and Dock Contract Revenue from Federal Government

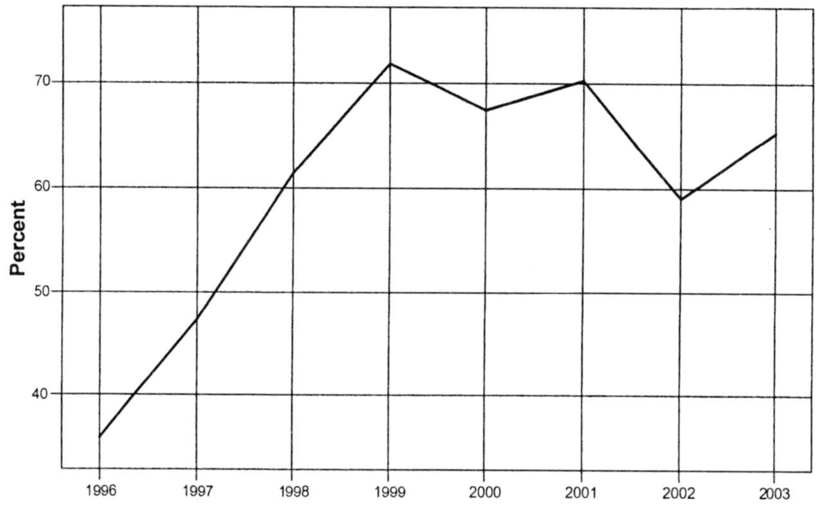

Source: Annual Reports to SEC

Perhaps just as significant in increasing the number of dredging projects is the law's provision requiring cost sharing. It called for a 75 percent to 25 percent cost sharing on dredging projects where the federal government contributed the 75 percent and the state or local government contributed the 25 percent. The benefit of cost sharing to the industry is something Great Lakes Dredge and Dock acknowledges in it annual reports (Great Lakes Dredge and Dock Corporation: Annual Report Pursuant to Section 13 and 15(d) of the Securities and Exchange Commission 2003, 3).

John Myers served on the House Appropriations Committee for nearly thirty years when Newt Gingrich jilted him when the Republicans took over Congress. As one of the senior most Republicans on the House Appropriations Committee, Myers anticipated being named chair of the Appropriations Committee in 1995. Instead, Newt Gingrich named Bob Livingston, whom Speaker Gingrich considered less accommodating to Democrats than Myers to chair the committee (Barone, Ujifusa, and Cohen 1997, 544). During his last term in office Myers was allowed to chair the Energy and Water Development Subcommittee. Myers retired from Congress at the end of the 104th Congress, but not before sponsoring the Energy and Water Appropriations Act of 1996. After thirty years of service, Congressman Myers retired to become a lobbyist with Dawson and Associates, a full service Government Relations Firm" (Dawson and Associates, Inc. 2004). The firm boasts that its strength...

> is an experienced, bipartisan team of former top-level government officials and policy experts. Our principals combine their experience and knowledge with an understanding of Legislative and Executive Branch processes and network of contacts to deliver results (Dawson and Associates, Inc. 2004).

And one of these top-level officials was John T. Myers who, according to lobbying documents filed with the Senate, would lobby on behalf of the Great Lakes Dredge and Dock Company for 20,000 dollars (Lobbying Report for Dawson and Associates 1999). By 2000, The Great Lakes Dredge and Dock Corporation would be paying Dawson and Associates 40,000 dollars for lobbying efforts (Lobbying Report for Dawson and Associates 2000).

Myers would not be the only former member of Congress to lobby for Great Lakes Dredge and Dock. Tom Bevill, the Democratic Congressman from Alabama retired in 1998 from the House of Representatives. Before doing so, however he had served as the chair of the Energy and Water Development Subcommittee. The Dawson and Associates Web Page reports of Bevill, "He had extensive responsibility for the funding of energy research programs, water resources development projects of the Corps of Engineers and other agencies, and other public works" (2004). Mr. Bevill, like Mr. Myers headed up the subcommittee that oversees the Army Corps of Engineers, which is responsible for determining fair dredging prices and then calling for bids.[5] The lobbying firm of Dawson and Associates boasts not two, but three former chairs of the Energy and Water Development Subcommittee of the Appropriations Committee. Not only do Congressmen Bevill and Myers appear as lobbyists for Dawson and associates, so to does Congressman H.L. Callahan who retired from Congress in 2000. Dawson and Associates writes of Congressman Callahan:

> In 2000, he became the chairman of the House Appropriations Subcommittee on Energy and Water Development. This Subcommittee is responsible for funding all civil projects of the U. S. Army Corps of Engineers as well as portions of the Department of the Interior, the Department of Energy and a number of independent agencies. In this position, congressman Callahan worked closely with the Bush Administration to develop and finance a new national energy policy. In addition to holding the chairmanship of the Energy and Water Development Appropriations Subcommittee, he also

served as Vice Chairman of Foreign Operations and as a member of the Transportation Subcommittee. Callahan's ability to get things done in congress enabled him to bring home millions of dollars in Federal funding for projects throughout south Alabama (Dawson and Associates 2004).

These three former members of Congress, along with a number of other former executive branch officials make up the lobbying team at Dawson and Associates and the Great Lakes Dredge and Dock Corporation.

It is worth noting that none of these three former lawmakers (Myers, Bevill and Callahan) received campaign contributions from employees of the Great Lakes Dredge and Dock Corporation. Out of some thirty-seven campaign contributions made between 1994 and 2004 by individuals employed by the Great Lakes Dredge and Dock Corporation, none were made directly to these post-congressional lobbyists with Dawson and Associates. The biggest recipients on campaign contributions from the Great Lakes Dredge and Dock Corporation have been Richard Durbin, having received nine contributions, Pete Visclosky with six, Robert Menendez with five, and Phil Gramm with four (Center for Responsive Politics 2004a). Figure 5.4 shows the total dollar amount contributed to federal candidates by the employees of Great Lakes Dredge and Dock.[6] The two spikes in 1996 and 2003 coincide with the positive Energy and Water Development Appropriations Act of 1996 and the uncertainty associated with efforts on the part of Citigroup Venture Capital to sell the company. The Great Lakes Dredge and Dock's Political Action Committee has only recently become a larger contributors. Although not reported in Figure 5.4, PAC contributions from the Great Lakes Dredge and Dock Company are worth mentioning. In 1998, the Great Lakes Dredge and Dock PAC contributed a mere 3,600 dollars to federal candidates (Center for Responsive Politics 2004a). The Center for Responsive Politics reports that in 2000, 2002 and 2004, the Great Lakes Dredge and Dock PAC contributed 20,700, 20,000 and 21,250 respectively.

Figure 5.4: Annual Campaign Contributions Made by Great Lakes Dredge and Dock Corporation Employees (1994-2004)

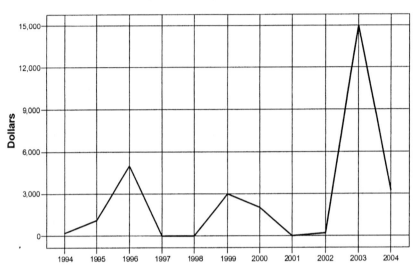

Source: Center for Responsive Politics

Glenn English and the Rural Electric Cooperative

Congressman Glenn English represented Oklahoma's sixth congressional district as a Democrat until he left office in 1993 at the age of 53. He had been in office since 1974, representing parts of Oklahoma City. He represented a mixed group of working-class whites and African-Americans. Although a Democrat, Congressman English tended to have a slightly more conservative voting record than his fellow Democrats. During his last term in office he was the fourth highest-ranking Democrats on the Agriculture Committee, and the chair of the Conservation, Credit and Rural Development Subcommittee. Congressman English was an active lawmaker during the 102nd Congress, sponsoring some twenty-three bills, and being successful in ensuring that four of those twenty-three bills become laws. During his final term – the 103rd – he was, in some ways, just as successful, if not more so.

At issue was the revamping of the Rural Electrification Administration (REA). REA was an overly bureaucratic government agency created by executive order by President Franklin D. Roosevelt as part of the country's efforts to improve the quality of life for rural Americans. REA was charged by the Agriculture Department to provide rural communities low interest loans for the purpose of bringing electricity and telephone services to these communities.

By the 1970s, almost every farming community had electricity (Brown 1980). And, by the late 1980s it was clear that the program's utility had expired. Still, the agency had strong support from lawmakers from rural communities. One of these strong advocates was Congressman Glenn English. Congressman English fought measures to weaken or abolish the agency, but in the end changes were made. Congressman Enrique De la Garza, along with Congressman Glenn English and two other lawmakers sponsored H.R. 3123, which was signed into law by President Bill Clinton on November 1, 1993. The Rural Electrification Loan Restructuring Act of 1993 changed several important parts of the REA. One thing that it did was to increase the interest rates on loans. The REA charged rural electric cooperatives an interest rate of 2 percent. The new law would increase those rates to 5 and 7 percent (P.L. 103-129, Sec.2).

Even though President Clinton had identified the Rural Electric Administration as a target for possible cuts or even elimination, the best that could be done with the REA was to consolidate some of its functions with other government agencies under the Agriculture Department (Michaelis, 1993, 1803). Glenn English has been a defender of small government programs stating, "In some ways it's because they were small. It makes them easy politically because they really didn't have much of a constituency.... It was easy to gang up on them" (Benenson 1993, 2884). Glenn English was not only successful at fending off the closing of the REA, he was also able to insure that rural electrical cooperatives would be able to apply for loans for water and waste development (Congressional Quarterly Weekly Report 1993, 2549). Able to win additional federal subsidies for the rural electric cooperatives, Congressman Glenn English resigned from Congress a month after President Clinton signed the bill into law (Borders and Dockery 1995, 15). He left Congress only to quickly take a job as the Chief Executive Officer of the National Rural Electric Cooperative Association (NRECA). Congressman Glenn English would not wait for his term to end to start his new job as a lobbyist for the NRECA.[7] One Democratic congressional aide reported, "English is a Smart guy, but he is not being hired because of his expertise on electrical cooperatives" (Harbison 1993, 3).

As the Chief Executive Officer for the National Rural Electric Cooperative Association, Congressman Glenn English has been quite successful. He writes, "The electric cooperative network is stronger today than it has ever been. Working together we have strengthened the bond of trust with the consumers we serve" (English 2002). And indeed it has become stronger. In its 2002 annual report the NRECA boasts having secured "a near record high $4 billion dollars in funding for the Rural Utilities Service (RUS) loan program" (2002, 8). The functions of the association have also increased in recent years. The NRECA writes:

Over time, as electric cooperatives have become more involved in the economic and community lives of their consumer-owners, NCERA's legislative, legal and regulatory agenda has evolved at their direction to embrace hundreds of issues affecting electric utility generation, transmission and distribution; energy policy and the environment; finance and tax matters; telecommunications; jobs creation; federal disaster assistance; the cooperative business model and governance; and consumer protections (NRECA 2002, 6).

The growth in functions of the NRECA reflects its political success. The NRECA'S political action committee, the Action Committee for Rural Electrification, "ranks 48th among the nation's 3,800 PACs" (NRECA 2002, 9). And even the NRECA is a significant contributor, having raised an estimated 1.6 million dollars and contributed 773,395 dollars to federal candidates (Center for Responsive Politics 2004a).

The National Rifle Association and Harold Volkmer

In the mid 1980s, Congressman Harold Volkmer, a Democrat from Missouri sponsored a bill that would revise the Gun Control Act of 1968. The Gun Control Act of 1968 regulated the interstate sale of guns, as well as regulated gun dealerships. The policy had been seen as onerous by the gun industry, and a violation of the second amendment to the US Constitution. So, in February of 1985 Congressman Volkmer sponsored House Bill 945. The bill aimed to weaken the 1968 law, which was passed in response to the assassinations of Martin Luther King and Robert Kennedy. States with strong support for gun ownership and the gun industry labored to weaken the legislation.

In the Senate, James McClure, Republican from Idaho, sponsored a similar bill – Senate bill 49, which would eventually become the law. Senator McClure did not have as much difficulty in getting his bill through the Senate as Congressman Volkmer had in the House. Chairing the House Judiciary Committee was Volkmer's fellow Democrat New Jersey Congressman Peter Rodino. Given that New Jersey is a more urban state where guns are used in the commission of crime with greater frequency than in more rural states, Congressman Rodino steadfastly refused to allow Congressman Volkmer's bill out of committee. Under the circumstance, most bills simply die in committee; but thanks in part to changes to the House rules, chairpersons could be forced to let a bill out of committee through the use of the discharge petition. In order for the bill to be let out of committee for the House to vote on, 218 House members would have to sign a petition calling on the for the bill to be brought to the floor. While the discharge petition is rarely successful, this would be one of those occasions when it would be successful in bringing a bill to the House floor.

Republican Congressman William Whitehurst, from Virginia picks up the story from here:

> Volkmer, however, had a powerful ally in the NRA. Its computers spat out thousands of letters to NRA members, urging them to write to their respective representatives requesting them to sign Volkmer's discharge petition and get his bill to the floor. Knowing that discharge petitions seldom get 218 signatures, many members decided that they would have their cake and eat it. They would sign the discharge petition, believing that it would suffer the fate of so many others and therefore not have to vote on Volkmer's bill, which was bottled up in the Judiciary Committee. They would then write to their NRA constituents and gratify them by declaring that they had signed the petition as requested. It seemed like a clever political ploy, only the problem was that too many of their colleagues decided to do the same thing and Volkmer quickly got within reach of the magic 218 signature (Whitehurst 2001, 217).

Congressman Rodino and others, seeing that their strategy to suppress the bill would not work, quickly offered their own bill, but they were too late. Whitehurst recalls that some of those who signed the petition regretted having done so, but by this point it was too late. Making matters difficult for these members of Congress was that on the day that they voted on the bill, law enforcement officials from throughout the country formed lines leading up to the chamber. Police officers in uniform pleaded with the members of the House not to vote for the McClure-Volkmer Bill. Whitehurst recalls the response of one of his colleagues when it was suggested that he simply remove his name off the petition, "I can't. I signed that damned discharge petition, and I'm afraid to have the NRA on my back" (Whitehurst 2001, 218).

The Firearms Owners' Protection Act (FOPA) would dramatically change the direction of gun regulations in the country, overturning years of court rulings (Hardy 1986). In the process of reducing regulations on the sales of guns, FOPA created what is referred to by some as the Gun Show Loophole, which allows individuals without Federal Firearms Licenses to sell guns without having to conduct a background check, while those dealers with Federal Firearms Licenses are required to conduct background checks. Gun shows allow individuals who may not be able to pass a background check when attempting to purchase a firearm an opportunity to purchase a gun without having their background checked.[8]

Congressman Volkmer served in the House until his retirement in 1996. That same year, at the Democratic Party's national convention, Volkmer walked out on Sarah Brady's antigun speech.[9] Since leaving office, Harold Volkmer has remained active in the political arena and on gun issues. He has been elected to serve on the National Rifle Association's board, and is registered as a lobbyist with the NRA. In his 2002 Lobbying Report, Volkmer reports that he will be lobbying on the specific issue of "HR2037, [the] Stearns - John Bill and in general issues favorable to individual right to keep and bear arms under the second amendment to the Constitution" (Lobbying Report for Harold Volkmer 2002). Volkmer has reported lobbying income for work done on behalf of the Institute for Legislative Action/National Rifle Association in which he makes some 80,000 dollars per year (see Lobbying Report for Harold Volkmer 1998-2002). Having worked so closely with the National Rifle Association while in office, Congressman Volkmer continues to work closely with the NRA as a lobbyist.

Tobacco and Senator Ford

Senator Wendell Ford was elected to serve the people of Kentucky in the US Senate in the mid 1970s, and he served in that position until the late 1990s. Senator Ford worked hard to protect tobacco interests from government encroachment. "Ford has worked hard on tobacco issues, from his first term when he got cigarettes excluded from the Consumer Product Safety Act to the Clinton years when he fought hard against the tobacco tax proposal to finance the Clinton healthcare plan" (Barone, Ujifusa and Cohen 1995, 542). The 1990s in particular were a bad decade for the tobacco industry. A combination of lawsuits, and changes in local, state and federal policy weakened the industry significantly. While the work of Morton Levin, showing a connection between smoking and lung cancer was published in 1950, the impact of the connection between tobacco and lung cancer on public policy would occur much later. The weakening began somewhat gradually, with the banning of smoking in airplanes, restaurants and other public places; as well as the placing of limits on advertisements, especially those directed at children.

In 1994, the head of the Food and Drug Administration (FDA) David Kessler announced plans to treat tobacco as a drug. He would quickly hear from Congress. One hundred twenty-four members of the House of Representatives and a third of the Senate sent a letter to the FDA complaining that efforts to ban tobacco could cost thousands of jobs. These members of Congress who signed the letter tended to be bigger recipients of tobacco money than those who did not sign the letter (Dreyfuss 1996). Commissioner Kessler would later recall:

> It was January 1995, the day of the close of the comment period, and we were prepared to handle millions of pages of comments—we knew we were going to get flooded. It was part of the industry's strategy to flood us with paper. I was prepared for all that. The one thing that I was not prepared for was 34 U.S. Senators opposing what we were doing. That was the industry flexing its muscle. What I didn't know at the time was that there were only 34. I mean, that was the best they could do. But when there are 34, you take notice. The

other thing I found striking was that the financial power also extended within the state and local legislatures. You could see campaigns—same letters, same paragraphs—and they were coming from state legislatures. Again, the extent of the campaign contributions and the industry trying to exert pressure on state legislatures to do battle with us was also evident; it was not just at the federal level (Center for Public Integrity 1998).

Responding to the efforts of the FDA, Senator Wendell Ford would say, "I believe nothing less than complete prohibition is good enough for the regulators over at the FDA and the anti-tobacco zealots," (Gleick and Bloch 1996, 54-55). For years Senator Ford worked to protect the tobacco industry from regulation that might undermine the industry. Repeatedly tobacco exemptions where placed on policies that attempted to protect the public and consumers, and repeatedly, Senator Ford fought them off. In an interview with the Center for Public Integrity's Charles Lewis, Charles, David Kessler expressed his frustration.

Charles Lewis: One of the things I'm most intrigued by is that there seems to have been no law by Congress to do anything regarding the regulation of tobacco after 1938, until you started bringing up at least the idea of regulation in the '90s.

David Kessler: It even goes to what Congress did—exempt tobacco on behalf of the industry. It passed laws to exempt tobacco from over a dozen federal consumer-protection statutes. TOSCA [Toxic Substances Control Act], the Consumer Product Safety Commission—there are dozens of acts that specifically exempted tobacco (Center for Public Integrity 1998).

The United States Supreme Court would further frustrate the FDA. In Food and Drug Administration, et al., Petitioners v. Brown and Williamson Tobacco Corporation et al., the court ruled that the FDA had not been given authority to regulate tobacco.

In this case, we believe that Congress has clearly precluded the FDA from asserting jurisdiction to regulate tobacco products. Such authority is inconsistent with the intent that Congress has expressed in the FDCA's overall regulatory scheme and in the tobacco-specific legislation that it has enacted subsequent to the FDCA. In light of this clear intent, the FDA's assertion of jurisdiction is impermissible (2000).

The Supreme Court essentially nullified the Food and Drug Administration's efforts to regulate tobacco. Since this time, attempts have been made by

Congress to provide the FDA the authority, but Congress has fallen short of doing so.

In spite of the setback to the FDA, the days of the small tobacco farmer have been numbered. Improvements in technology, in conjunction with a decline in the number of smokers have weakened many small farmers. Perhaps foreseeing the plight of small farmers, Senator Ford introduced the idea of buying out small farmers while at the same time getting rid of tobacco quotas. During the Great Depression, Franklin D. Roosevelt promised farmers that if they agreed to tobacco production quotas, the federal government would guarantee tobacco prices. By the late 1990s the quotas set by the government had been reduced significantly, and small tobacco farmers were suffering as a consequence.

In an attempt to undo the effects of the Agricultural Adjustment Act of 1938, Senator Wendell Ford suggested a buyout for the small tobacco farmer in 1997. In 1997, Senator Ford sponsored Senate Bill 1310. The bill called for the revitalization of tobacco communities, payments to tobacco farmers, provided educational opportunities for those affected by the loss of price supports, and immunity from lawsuits. The proposal would have provided 28.5 billion dollars to be spent over ten years to help tobacco communities recover from the loss of government support (Carroll 2004). The bill was referred to the Committee on Agriculture, but never came up for a floor vote. At about the same time, Senator Ford, attempting to get in front of the assault on tobacco, also sponsored Senate Bill 201, which would limit advertising to children. President Bill Clinton would make it clear that the federal government was not out to ban tobacco, just the advertising to young people. Speaking In Carrollton Kentucky, President Clinton would thank Senator Ford:

> The first thing I'd like to do is to say a special word of appreciation to Wendell Ford. His work on the tobacco bill that's now moving through the Senate I think has been very valuable in trying to provide clear and certain protection to tobacco farmers, to warehouses, to communities without compromising our long-term goal of reducing teen smoking (Clinton, 1998 612).

The message was to reassure tobacco farmers that they were not the targets of the Federal government.

Senator Ford's bills were not successful at becoming laws, but neither were the FDAs efforts. Undermining the efforts to regulate tobacco was the tobacco industry's increased spending on lobbyists and on politicians. When David Kessler joined the FDA he did not believe that the industry was very strong, or at least that its credibility with the public was such that no one would believe the testimony of the industry. "Their public credibility was nonexistent, but the money was so powerful, and it was money all over Washington. They literally could buy anything; they could hire anyone" (Center for Public Integrity 1998).

Figure 5.5: Tobacco Campaign Contributions

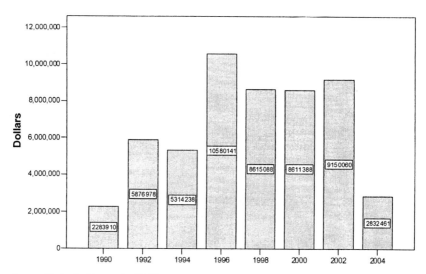

Source: Center for Responsive Politics

The Figure 5.5 shows dollar amounts contributed by the tobacco industry to federal campaigns in the millions of dollars. The figure shows a dramatic increase in the amount of campaign spending from 1994 to 1996. It was during this period that David Kessler began to suggest that the FDA had the authority to regulate tobacco. For the next several election cycles, the tobacco industry maintained relatively high levels of spending on political campaigns. One of the big recipients was Senator Wendell Ford, receiving 76,148 dollars from tobacco in 1996 according to the Center for Responsive Politics. He was the top recipient in the Senate in 1992 and 20th in 1998 (Center for Responsive Politics 2004b). But by 2004, the worst was over, and campaign spending had returned to pre-Kessler levels.

In 1998, however, the story for the tobacco industry had been much bleaker. The tobacco industry's powerful lobbying arm – the Tobacco Institute – was shut down after the tax-exempt status of the organization was brought into question. Then a more fractured lobbying effort followed. After years of fighting FDA efforts to regulate the industry, Philip Morris, which had the resources to hire its own in-house lobbyists, began to lobby Congress to allow the FDA to regulate tobacco. Recognizing that Philip Morris is the only cigarette manufacturer that is powerful enough to implement and survive FDA regulations, the other cigarette makers objected. Steve Watson, a Lorillard Vice-President described a Philip Morris backed bill to regulate the industry as, "little more than a 'Marlboro Monopoly Act'" (Carey 2001, 43).

After three decades of public service Senator Wendell Ford retired from Congress. But he would not be gone for good. He would reappear as a lobbyist with Dickstein, Shapiro, Morin and Oshinsky in 2000. The United States Senate Office of Public Records shows Senator Ford has continued to be active lobbying on behalf of the tobacco industry. Lorillard, the Pipe Tobacco Council, the Smokeless Tobacco Council, and the Cigar Association of America are some of his clients. Lorillard has paid Dickstein, Shapiro, Morin and Oshinsky one million dollars to lobby on its behalf (Lobbying Reports for Dickstein, Shapiro, Morin and Oshinsky 2004).

What was so difficult to enact while in the Senate, Senator Ford helped to make law as a lobbyist. In the fall of 2004, President George W. Bush signed into law a corporate tax overhaul bill named "The American Jobs Creation Act of 2004". Among other things, the bill provided for a 10 billion dollar buy-out of tobacco farmers' quotas over the next ten years. Although the 10 billion dollars is considerably less than what Senator Wendell Ford attempted to provide in the late 1990s, it will achieve some of the same goals – it will help small farmers get out of the business of growing tobacco. "The little guys won't survive this." Said one small farmer, reacting to the news of the buyout said, "Unfortunately, I'm one of the little guys" (Jonsson 2004, 1). Appearing as items 35 through 38 on the Lobbying Activity sheet for Senator Ford's client Lorillard Tobacco is the American Jobs Creating Act of 2004 (Lobbying Reports for Dickstein, Shapiro, Morin and Oshinsky 2004). The lobbying firm that Senator Ford would become a lobbyist for would be successful at lobbying for the American Jobs Creation Act, which among other things enacted the buyout for tobacco farmers.

Conclusion

This chapter provides examples of the connection between the public policy that former members of Congress sponsored while in office and the special interest groups that they would go to work for while out of office. These case studies demonstrate a connection between what the former lawmakers did while in office and what they did out of office. While there are many other cases that one could have shown, I opted to focus just on five. This ought not be taken to mean that there are not other connections. As stated in the beginning of this chapter, some connections are much more evident than others. The connections between the policy and the special interest groups that benefit from the policy are made more evident in this chapter. One might be quite correct in stating that former members of Congress are policy experts, and clearly, that expertise is valuable to lobbying organizations and interest groups. Some of the lawmakers highlighted above were lifelong supporters of the special interest groups that they would represent later in life. These individuals like many others did not become supporters for these special interest groups during their last term in office. They nurtured these relationships over many years and showed a willingness to fight for these interest groups. These groups often times represented big employers in the representatives' districts. At other times, these interests focused on policy areas where the lawmakers had become leaders on the subject. What we find in these five case studies is evidence that material benefits are exchanged, flowing from the public sector to the private sector, and it is the policy maker who is the connection between the two. The policy maker is assisting in the creation of policy that benefits special interest groups, and these special interest groups, whether intentional or not, are rewarding those individuals who facilitated favorable policy with post-congressional employment as lobbyists.

---

[1] It should be noted that when talking about laws, I am excluding all joint resolutions, concurrent resolutions and amendments.

[2] Paragraph "i" reads, "Authorization of Appropriations.--Section 10311 of such Act (as redesignated by subsection (e)(1)) (20 U.S.C. 8067) is amended by striking ``$15,000,000 for fiscal year 1995'' and inserting ``$100,000,000 for fiscal year 1999''''.

[3] See the Charter Schools Development Corporation's WebPages at http://www.csdc.org/about/.

[4] Gross profit is the difference between contract revenue and cost of contract revenue. I report this rather than stock price because it best captures the company's business activity. The data is found in two annual reports to the SEC. These are the 2000 report and the 2004 report.

[5] Lester Edelman, former Chief Council for the US Army Corps of Engineers also lobbies with Dawson and Associates on behalf of Great Lakes Dredge and Dock. This is reported on the Senate Lobbying Disclosure form signed by Robert Dawson on July 17th, 2000, and given the House identification number 34231009. It is found at http://sopr.senate.gov/cgi-win/opr_gifviewer.exe?/2000/01/000/322/000322134|2.

[6] It should be noted that the campaign contributions listed in the figure do not include PAC contributions.

[7] The Senate Office of Public Records shows that as late as 2003 Glenn English was registered as a lobbyist for the NRECA. See http://sopr.senate.gov/.

[8] Some evidence has suggested that restrictions on gun purchases – waiting period requirements and licensing requirements – may be connected to reductions in gun-related violence (Kwon, Scott, Safranski, and Bae 1997).

[9] Sarah Brady is the wife of James Brady, Ronald Reagan's Press Secretary who was shot and left partially paralyzed when John Hinckley Jr. attempted to assassinate President Reagan. The Brady Bill, which calls for a five day waiting period on the purchase of a handgun is named after Mr. Brady.

6

Post-congressional Lobbying, National Security and Institutional Legitimacy

Members of Congress have now come to covet what was once the unseemly work of lobbying. Lobbying on the part of former members of Congress was once the alternative for those members who were defeated in their reelections bids but preferred not to return to their rural communities. Post-congressional lobbying has now become the next step for many public servants. It is the step that, for many, insures a much-improved income and a less taxing schedule. It is now commonplace for the most senior and high-ranking government officials to land careers as lobbyists. A profession that was once viewed with some disdain on the part of elected officials is now revered. Barring any significant change in the way that Washington works, one can expect a couple of patterns to continue to emerge. One of these is that former elected officials enter and exit public service with greater frequency adding a new dimension to the concept of the iron triangle. The antiquated notion of iron triangles has been displaced in recent years by issue networks, but perhaps the displacement of the theory of the iron triangle has come too soon. The iron triangle needs to be revisited, adding a new "spin" to the theory. We are seeing the actors in the iron triangle – the members of Congress, the lobbyists, and the bureaucrats – taking turns in each other's seats.

In the process, public policy suffers. One might speculate that innovation and creativity are stifled when the policy making process is limited to one group of individuals who are creating public policy. These individuals may unwittingly serve as the guardians of the status quo, undermining the implementation of new ideas. Because the policy maker and the lobbyist is the same person, that person's predispositions for one policy position can have the effect of preventing the presentation of an alternative policy position. This problem is compounded by the power and respect that is afforded to members of

Congress and former members of Congress. Many often defer to policy makers out of reverence, and thus give needless value to ideas that otherwise would not merit them. Policy alternatives that do not have the support of the lawmaker or former lawmaker may never be given the opportunity to compete effectively with policy positions espoused by powerful members of Congress-turned-lobbyists. Congressman Jay Dickey, Republican from Arkansas, gained notoriety in the mid-1990s for sponsoring what is often referred as the Dickey Amendment, which prohibited the use of federal dollars for research that would destroy human embryos 45 C. F. R. 46.208(a)(2) and 42 U. S. C. § 289g. This was an amendment that was added to an appropriations bill for the Department of Health and Human Services. In 2000, Congressman Dickey was defeated for reelection by Mike Ross, an Arkansas Democrat. After an unsuccessful attempt to regain the seat he lost in 2002, Jay Dickey reappeared as a lobbyist for Welch Resources Incorporated. He continues to lobby on matters of healthcare appropriations (United States Senate Office of Public Records 2004). While his role may have been muted somewhat now that he is no longer a member of Congress, he continues to keep guard in areas of public policy that deal with women and children's health in the United States and in the third world.

Competition for new policy is further diminished because former members of Congress are afforded many more benefits that non-former members of Congress are afforded. "The line between a congressman and a former congressman is pretty thin," states former congressman Wendell Bailey from Missouri, "You can pretty much do anything a congressman can do except vote" (Murphy, 1999, A1). Ex-lawmakers are much more likely to get access to one of their former colleagues than other lobbyists. "I don't have to buy my way into the office by being a campaign contributor or taking their staffs out for endless lunches," Jack Buechner said. "You may not win, but you get your time in office. That's the critical part" (Murphy 1999 A1). And, as a lobbyist, a former member of Congress is provided extraordinary access. Former lawmakers are in a position to interact with current members of Congress in settings that other lobbyists are not allowed to participate. In 2003, the Washington Post ran the following story:

> Rep. Zach Wamp (R-Tenn.) had just finished his treadmill run in the House gym in July when he spotted a former colleague, Jay Dickey, walking over from playing paddleball. Dickey, who started his own lobbying firm in January, handed Wamp a paper containing legislative language that a client was seeking from the Appropriations Committee, on which Wamp serves. Dickey's business card was attached. "I said, 'Take this slip of paper to a staffer, and I'll get back to you,'" recalled Dickey, an Arkansas Republican trying to win federal funding for a river navigation project on behalf of a Pine Bluff, Ark., sand and gravel company.

Most lobbyists would kill for the chance to place a client's highly sought proposal in a lawmaker's hand. For Dickey and other former members of Congress, it is fairly easy. In a town in which access often translates into influence, former members of Congress have several advantages, from free parking spots on Capitol grounds to the ability to mingle with lawmakers and their aides in cloakrooms and private committee rooms.

Although many former staffers, administration officials and political aides have flourished as lobbyists, they lack the edge enjoyed by those who have served in Congress. Moreover, according to several congressional aides, some of these former lawmakers are increasingly bold in using their access for lobbying, a scenario that troubles public watchdog groups.

Several lawmakers-turned-lobbyists say they are careful not to abuse their congressional privileges. There is no doubt, however, that they belong to a special club. Former members can roam the Capitol without passing through traditional security checks, attend the Senate's weekly Democratic and Republican strategy lunches, and walk onto the House or Senate floor. As a professional courtesy, they can get appointments with former colleagues almost automatically.

During a recent House Transportation and Infrastructure Committee bill-drafting session, Dickey hovered behind the dais and persuaded Rep. Gene Taylor (D-Miss.) to show him a copy of the proposed legislation, to make sure it would authorize work on the Arkansas River project that the Pine Bluff Sand and Gravel Co. wanted. The company paid Dickey $40,000 in lobbying fees during the first six months of the year, according to public records (Remer 2003).

This story captures the tremendous advantage that former members of Congress have over their fellow lobbyists. Former members of Congress are allowed in places that other lobbyists are not allowed into. This provides former members of Congress a tremendous advantage in the competition for influence. The lobbying playing field is hardly equal.

It has not always been this way. Not too long ago, a major concern was that members of Congress were serving for very long periods of time. There were even attempts to set term limits for members of Congress. Although term limits were found to be unconstitutional by the US Supreme Court, term limits do remain popular in some sectors. Writing in the 1960s, Nelson Polsby was the first political scientist to argue that the US Congress had matured into an institution. As evidence of this, he pointed to the lengthening of congressional tenures (1968, 146-147). Throughout the latter half of the 20th century the length of congressional service grew considerably. For members of Congress, once elected, the position was semi-permanent. Redistricting led to the creation of less competitive congressional elections, which in the end benefited incumbents, lengthening their tenures. Realignments of the electorate (Fiorina, Rohde and Wissel 1975, Price 1975), changes in party competition (Brookshire and Duncan 1983), changes in congressional rules (Bullock and Loomis 1985), and the use of the federal bureaucracy to benefit constituents (Fiorina 1989) have all impacted the length of the congressional careers of members of Congress.

Ambitious members of Congress, wanting to maximize their political power served for longer periods of time during the later part of the 19th Century and throughout the 20th. Samuel Kernell has identified political ambition as being "the primary contributor to increased membership stability" in the 19th Century (Kernell 1977 669). Those members of Congress who entered politics early in life were particularly more likely to make a career of politics (Schlesinger 1966, 176). They were also choosing politics as their first career choice, while others who would enter politics later in life tended to enter politics "due to failure in some other endeavor" (Schlesinger 1966, 176). Those who entered politics early in life were much more likely to identify themselves as politicians, while those who entered politics later in life continued to identify themselves by their previous profession (Loomis 1984, 540). Those who entered politics early also brought some detriments with them. Congressman Bill Frenzel, stated in a 1997 interview with Jeff Shear:

> My own judgment is that since 1974 we have been electing different kinds of Congressmen with great ability and almost no experience. Occasionally you get a Gordon Smith who will come out of a state legislature, but mostly you're getting guys off the street, as you did in 1974. Some of them not only have not met a payroll or served in the legislature; some of them have not even been *on* a payroll. By and large, I think their capability is probably better than some of the folks I remember in Congress when I first started, but clearly their experience and their knowledge are way behind (Center for Public Integrity 1997a).

Those who entered politics early in life were more likely to come form the ranks of the legal profession, while those who entered politics later in life came from the ranks of the business community (Schlesinger 1966, 177-179). It is among those who enter politics later in life that one can see more focused ambitions. Joseph Schlesinger writes:

> In terms of the age at which they received their major nomination, the early starters run behind many of the older starters; a higher proportion of those entering public office in their early forties achieve their nomination before the age of 55 than those who have started their careers in their early twenties (1966, 182).

One might speculate that those entering Congress later in life are more inclined to view their stay in the chamber as temporary and helpful in achieving some other career path. Loomis writes, "A House member with no presidential ambitions, not even in the midst of the longest night, may develop them once elected to the Senate" (1984, 540).

But the environment has changed since the 1970s. Freshman members of Congress are increasingly as powerful as some of their more senior colleagues. One member of Congress is quoted as saying, "Most members these days have as much power in their second term as they will in their eight, so what is there to look forward to?" (Hibbing1982b, 94). Although this was said well over twenty years ago, it holds true today, even more so, as junior members of Congress leapfrog in front of more senior colleagues who are viewed as not being ideological enough, or having the stamina for more powerful positions. Seniority has lost its value:

> In the old days, a member with 8 or 10 years of service was very reluctant to retire because he was throwing away years of stored capital, dues paying or whatever you want to call it. Now 8 or 10 years means nothing. You're not giving up much by retiring because you might have been denied your chair even if you had seniority. Why stay? (Hibbing1982b, 94).

Replacing seniority is a combination of competence, vigor and loyalty to the party. As some members of Congress reach the peak of political power earlier than in the past, they are seeking other forms of power. Many are moving to the news media where they can continue to influence policymakers via their constituents. Susan Molinari, for instance, who was a rising star in the Republican Party left almost as quickly as she arrived serving only six years in Congress. She left to host *CBS News Saturday Morning*. John Kasich who served a bit longer in Congress also left the House to host the Fox program *From the Heartland with John Kasich*. As has been made clear in this book, many others leave to become lobbyists. Hale Boggs, the partner with Patton-Boggs has suggested that increasingly members of Congress are viewing the lobbying profession with longing, preferring "to be him [the lobbyists] than me [the member of Congress]"(Center for Public Integrity 1997b).

The devaluing of seniority has meant that the House of Representatives is attracting members with greater concern for specific agendas than for the wellbeing of the institution. This is the perception conveyed by Congressman Frenzel who sees members entering the institution for the purpose of making war, rather than public policy (Center for Public Integrity 1997a). Congressman Frenzel continues:

> When you start making war, either from the right or the left, it's hard
> to be friendly with your adversaries. I think the Members have sort of
> built their own environment, which is a very unpleasant one. But
> that's what they want to do. They all say, "Well, I'm not going to be
> here very long and I've got very important things to do, so I can't
> screw around with comity or amenities. I just got to get the job
> done." I think that makes for a very difficult environment (Center for
> Public Integrity 1997a).

This environment contributes to the disparagement of the institution. Service and representation seize to become the goals of service in Congress. Congress becomes a steppingstone to other, more profitable careers. Increasingly there is greater acceptance of viewing Congress as a steppingstone to other careers. There has been a growing tolerance among members of Congress for former colleagues to lobby Congress. This may be because current members see themselves as potential lobbyists or perhaps out of a genuine concern for wanting their former colleagues to do well in their new lives. Congressman William Whitehurst has recounted:

> A number of my former committee colleagues and staff members
> from the committee went on to serve as "consultants" for a myriad of
> defense contractors. Before I retired in January 1987, I was offered a
> similar opportunity by a former staff member of the Senate Armed
> Services Committee whom I had gotten to know and had occasionally
> seen socially. He assured me that I could make "well into six figures"
> in my first year with him, but I preferred to come home and resume
> teaching. I knew it would be less stressful and neither my wife nor I
> ever had what is known as "Potomac Fever," and obsession with
> Washington and all that goes on there.

> There is nothing wrong with former members of Congress going to
> work representing the business interests of a private concern, so long
> as the rules that govern all lobbying activities are observed. Some
> have been enormously successful, financially and otherwise, at it
> (Whitehurst 2001, 211).

This growing tolerance for post-congressional lobbying is contributing to increased boldness in the seeking of lobbying positions. The bold moves taken by Mary Bono and Billy Tauzin to land the coveted lobbying position with the Recording Industry of America only helps to highlight the growing tolerance for lobbying as a viable post-congressional career option. It was only after Lloyd Grove of the Washington Post made their bold auditioning for the position public,[1] that both stated they were not really seeking the job, which was eventually offered to former Agriculture Secretary Dan Glickman.

The boldness of pursing clients has extended to areas outside of the United States. Former members of Congress are being hired as foreign agents by other countries to represent those countries' interests in the United States. Many of these countries have well documented human rights violations. In 1992, the Center for Public Integrity issued a report entitled, *The Torturers' Lobby*. In it, the author, Pamela Brogan reports that lobbying firms were paid some 30 million dollars between 1991 and 1992 to lobby on the behalf of countries with questionable human rights records. The author goes on to claim that the American people indirectly subsidized the activities of these lobbyists (Brogan 1992). Other countries that former members of Congress have lobbied for have been known for being hostile to the United States. Still, these countries hire representatives to look out for their interest in the United States. Former members of Congress can boast that only someone like themselves – former members of Congress – can represent the interest of tyrannical regimes. Few other lobbyists would be allowed access to members of Congress if their clients had contemptible reputations, but because a lobbyist was once a member of Congress, that lobbyist is allowed an audience with current members of Congress. It should be noted that it is not uncommon for former members of Congress, like other high-ranking government officials, to register as foreign agents. The Foreign Agent Registration Act (FARA) was signed into law in 1938 for the purpose of identifying foreign agents that were attempting to influence public opinion or policymakers. This law was enacted under the concern that Germany might be influencing public opinion in the US during World War II. Since this time, hundreds of foreign entities and agents have registered with the Department of Justice, making it difficult for the Justice Department to keep abreast of the registrants. FARA has since been weakened further by the Lobbying Disclosure Act of 1995, which allows a certain class of lobbyists to register with the House and Senate. Unlike the rules set by FARA, the Lobbying Disclosure Act of 1995 "has no criminal sanctions" (Department of Justice 2004).

The list of former members of Congress turned-foreign agents reads like a who's who of American Government. Robert Dole, William Paxon, Robert Livingston, Steve Solarz, and many others have registered as foreign agents. These individuals have gone from representing their fellow Americans to representing foreign countries and entities. At times these individuals have take positions that run counter to those positions taken by their own government. In 1998, on national television on the Late Show with David Letterman, former Senator Robert Dole criticized the US position on the Taiwan-China problem (Abramson 1998). The position Dole criticized was one that would later be upheld by George W. Bush – a member of Robert Dole's own party (Milbank and Kessler 2003, 21A). The Taiwan-China problem is that China sees Taiwan as being part of China. Taiwan would like to see itself as being independent from

China. And, the United States has codified language that would call for the US to defend Taiwan if China ever attacked Taiwan. The three actors being economically and strategically interconnected would prefer to maintain peace and stability. The way to accomplish this has been a precarious agreement in which Taiwan simply does not declare independence from China. Not declaring independence from China keeps China from attacking, which in turn keeps the US from defending Taiwan. This has been the bedrock of the United States' *One-China policy.* Since Taiwan is pressured not to declare independence from China, it is seen as part of China. The Dole critique of US policy toward Taiwan and China did not summarily reveal that Dole was a foreign agent for Taiwanese interests[2].

As Senator Dole chastised the Clinton Administration for US policy toward Taiwan, Dole was no longer acting as a former member of the Senate, but as a paid representative for the people of Taiwan. While David Letterman's national audience may have viewed Senator Robert Dole as a statesman, one could argue that he was no longer acting as a statesman but as a foreign agent for Taiwan. The concern is more than misperception. The concern is that many former members of Congress, because of their longevity, and power while in office, maintain a significant amount of credibility and legitimacy. When former members of Congress trade on this credibility and legitimacy, their personal gain may come at the expense of American interests. While it could certainly be argued that many if not most of those who serve their fellow compatriots in government are truly patriotic individuals, loyalties, if not diminished, could be distorted by the pressures placed upon them by foreign clients. While less than two decades ago it was much easier to determine the difference between US interests and the interest of the enemy, i.e. communism and the threat of the Soviet Union in particular; the end of the Cold War has made it difficult for Americans to clearly distinguish where America's interests start and end.

With the end of the Cold War and the fragmentation of the former Soviet Union the United States has found itself the hegemonic superpower. As a consequence, nations have flocked to the US to attempt to influence policy as it relates to them. This growing effort to influence US policy has been exacerbated by the tumult around the world and in the US itself. Global economic downturns, growing terrorism in the US, and growing US military involvement abroad have all sent signals to other nations that it is to the United States that these countries must appeal to for their own development and safety. But, just as the end of the Cold War brought an end to the Soviet Union, the post-Cold War period has brought the rise of new challenges. Primary among these is the growing strength of countries like China and India, the planet's two most populous countries. China in particular has proven to be both a challenge and an opportunity for the United States. China is a major US trading partner, but its communist system coupled with human rights abuses and belligerent position over the issue of Taiwan have led to tension between China and the US.

Throughout much of the 1990s China lobbied for normalizing trade relations between the United States and China. Although it took some time to occur, China was successful in normalizing relations with the US, and eventually entering the World Trade Organization in 2001. Helping it along has been the United States' China Business Council, which has been instrumental in garnering support for US economic policies that benefit both American companies and China. The end of the Cold War however, had another impact. It also sharply decreased the world's demand for weapons. As a consequence, arms traders had to seek new markets for their wares (US General Accounting Office National Security and International Affairs Division 2000, 1). Arguably one of the most vibrant economies during much of the 1990s was that of China's. In recent years China has continued to consume a variety of products with a voracious appetite.

The demand for weapons and technology has not been an exception to this voracious appetite. A case in point has been the interaction between China and Hughes Electronics. In the late 1990s Hughes electronics was accused of sharing sensitive satellite technology with China. This was done during a time when the US was restricting the sharing of sensitive technology with the Chinese because China had sold missiles to Pakistan. Word of the commercial exchange between China and Hughes Electronics was revealed after a Chinese rocket carrying a Hughes built, Loral operated commercial satellite crashed.[3] The Washington Post quoted the Air Force Intelligence and the Defense Technology Security Administration, which investigated the incident as stating that Hughes electronics "went well beyond what should have been allowed" (Pincus and Mintz 1998, A22). Making the case for China was Congressman Toby Roth, a Wisconsin Republican. Congressman Roth sponsored several bills that would have relaxed restrictions on the sale of satellites to China. The Congressman served as chair of the House Foreign Affairs Committee's Subcommittee on Economic Policy, Trade and Environment at the time, thus, he was in a position to help such bills along. At the time Toby Roth was under pressure from Mike Armstrong, the head of Hughes Electronics. Toby Roth sought help to relax restrictions from National Security Adviser Anthony Lake (Mintz 1998, A04). Roth attempted to shift the decision of exporting communications satellite away from the State Department to the Secretary of Commerce (US House of Representatives Report 105-582, 1998, 37). It may have been expected that the Secretary of Commerce would have been less restrictive than the Secretary of State in authorizing such sales. While Congressman Roth's House Bill 104-361 was not enacted into law, both Bill Clinton and his predecessor waived the restrictions on the exportation of satellites to China thirteen times (US House of Representatives Report 105-582, 1998, 7). At times these relaxations of the rules came at the coaxing of the Congressman from Wisconsin. A price would be paid for the relaxation of the rules. Hughes and Boeing would later be fined 32 million dollars by the State Department for violating the Arms Export Control Act and the International Traffic in Arms Regulations. As part of the consent agreement, the two "companies are required to appoint special compliance officials who will be responsible for oversight of the companies' activities in China and the countries of the Former Soviet Union" (US Department of State, Office of the Spokesman 2003).

Congressman Toby Roth left Congress in 1997 to pursue a lobbying career. He formed the Roth Group, a lobbying firm that specialized in the exportation of high-tech equipment as well as tourism. Some of his major clients include Hughes Electronics, Boeing and the American League for Exports and Securities Assistance. Roth also lobbies for the American League for Exports and Securities Assistance (ALESA), which is a strong proponent of liberalized arms sales policies. In 2003, Roth lobbied for HR 1950 which would, among other things, "authorize appropriations under the Arms Export Control Act and the Foreign Assistance Act of 1961". The bill would also have revisited Roth's earlier concern of having the Secretary of Commerce involved in the decision to sell arms to arms embargoed countries. Section 1105 of the bill would have called for the Secretary of State to consult with the Secretary of Commerce in matters of arms sales to countries that the US has arms embargos against.

While it is generally assumed that what is good for corporate America is good for the country, there are certainly provisions of the law that do not always agree with such a position. The United States has placed arms embargoes on a number of countries for a variety of reasons. These countries may harbor terrorists, they may be ruled by regimes that wish the US or its allies harm, or they may be ruled by regimes that threaten America's interests. Concerns for national security are certainly of great importance to the US political leadership, but so too is commerce. The two – national security and commerce – often clash, as in the case with the sale of sensitive technology to China, a country that is both a major US trading partner and also a potential threat to US interests. Reconciling the two competing concerns is a challenge for the US, and clearly the US will not rely on a few corporate interests intent on selling weapons to China to dictate US policy. Nevertheless, the challenge is made all the more difficult when individuals that are in a position to create policy also work to lobby on behalf of interests impacted by that policy. A former member of Congress sponsoring bills on a subject like selling sensitive technology to China may be deferred to by colleagues under the assumption that the policy is sound and good for America. That same Congressman, no longer in office but lobbying on behalf of the same interest that would have benefited from the earlier policies, may continue to be deferred to by his former colleagues. One can envision a more experienced and thoughtful ex-lawmaker circumventing those colleagues from one committee that are as familiar with the issues as the ex-lawmaker in order to maximize the likelihood of getting a bill sponsored and enacted into law. A former lawmaker who served on the House's Foreign Affairs Committee may be wise, for instance, to lobby in favor of an unpopular interest in some other committee where members of this other committee may not be as opposed to the unpopular interest.

With the help of many former members of Congress, foreign entities have been very successful at extracting a variety of concessions from the United States. Congressman Whitehurst writes, "Foreign governments have had unusual success in either shaping American foreign policy in their favor, or securing a pipeline to our treasury, or both" (Whitehurst 2001, 212). In deed, the biggest recipients of US aid are countries with lobbyists who have been former members of Congress. Israel, Egypt and Turkey are among the biggest recipients of United States aid. They have also hired lobbying firms that were either founded by former members of Congress or who have been known to employ former members of Congress. The Livingston Group, which was founded by Congressman Robert Livingston, for example, has represented both Turkish and Israeli interests.

The success of many foreign governments and foreign entities in influencing US policy is driven by the ability of those countries' lobbyists to contribute money to candidates. In a 1997 analysis, the Center for Responsive Politics listed the seventeen largest foreign agent contributors to American Campaigns. Of these, three were former members of Congress – Thomas Downey, Thomas Evans, and Ray Kogovsek – while others represented firms where former members of Congress where senior partners (Daly, John 1997). The Center for Responsive Politics' *Open Secrets* web page reports that the Pro-Israeli groups contributed some 5.6 million dollars to both Democrats and Republicans (Center for Responsive Politics 2004c). The power of the pro-Israeli lobby is well known in Washington and can boast of having removed powerful members of Congress whose positions were inconsistent with those of the Israeli lobby. The Israeli lobby has been credited with helping to defeat Senators William Fulbright, Charles Percy and Roger Jepsen, while in the House, Congressmen Paul Findley and Paul McCloskey have both been defeated thanks in part to the role of the pro-Israeli lobby. Paul Findley would later credit the American Israel Public Affairs Committee (AIPAC) for his defeat. Findley would recall:

> In a report to a Jewish gathering in Austin, Texas, a few days after election day, Thomas A. Dine, the organization's executive director, said his forces brought 150 students from the University of Illinois to "pound the pavements and knock on doors" and concluded, "This is a case where the Jewish lobby made a difference. We beat the odds and defeated Findley." (Findley 1989, 22)

It is widely believed by members of Congress that opposition to AIPAC "can make or break their chances at election time" (Findley 1989, 25). Congressman Whitehurst similarly recalled the concern that AIPAC would raise in members of Congress. Whitehurst writes, "Thomas Dine was correct in his assessment of the importance that incumbent congressmen and senators attached to the power of AIPAC and associated lobbies" (Whitehurst 2001, 216). He recalled a story in the mid 1980s when several of his colleagues from Virginia contemplated a vote against the sale of weapons to Saudi Arabia. It was understood that this was a test to measure loyalty to Israel. Several of his colleagues voted against the sale, for fear of incurring the wrath of the Israeli lobby. Whitehurst would conclude, "While I regarded myself as a friend of the Israeli lobby, my oath had been taken to the US Constitution" (Whitehurst 2001, 216).

It should be noted that in the case of AIPAC, those who are registered as lobbyists are not former members of Congress, although AIPAC's board does include former member of Congress Rudy Boschwitz. There is however a fair number of former members of Congress who work for firms that represent the special interests of countries like Israel. Former Congressman Dick Armey who now works for Piper Rudnick as Senior Policy Advisor wrote recently, "Israeli companies and firms, with their long-standing experience in providing anti-terrorism products and services, offer an unparallel reservoir of experience that can and must be utilized to the advantage of both our countries" (2003, 2). Piper Rudnick also represents Israeli foreign entities in the US, representing Tefen Yazamot, an Israeli firm.

One lobbying firm that has taken full advantage of ex-lawmakers lobbying is Advantage Associates. While former members of Congress have been lobbying for years, Advantage Associates was the first lobbying firm that was founded by a group of former members of Congress in the late 1990s. Currently, Advantage Associates boasts twelve partners who are also former members of Congress. The Advantage Associates web page reports that "there is a tremendous advantage to being a former Member of Congress: access to key policymakers and leaders, a special understanding of the complex procedures involved, and an insider's knowledge of what is truly happening" (Advantage Associates 2004). Access is what Advantage Associates sells, and it sells it to, among other clients, other countries. A significant number of the partners are registered as foreign agents, doing work for other countries.

There is a growing tolerance among public officials to allow the revolving door to continue to revolve. As ex-policy makers leave office they return to lobby their old friends on behalf of special interests. The danger is that allowing ex-officials to lobby exposes the United States to the possibility that public policy created under the influence of these ex-lawmakers may not benefit the national interest. When ex-lawmakers are allowed to register as foreign agents, or even when they lobby on behalf of foreign governments' interests without registering as foreign agents, not only is the possibility that public policy created under the influence of these ex-lawmakers not in the national interest, it may be in the interest of foreign governments while compromising the interest of the American people. While elected officials take an oath to the United States, the allegiance sworn to under that oath is all to readily limited to the time period under which the public official serves as an elected official. But as the tolerance for post-congressional lobbying grows one can expect to see increased manipulation of public policy for personal gain. Seemingly unimportant text written into policy will be given new life by those who wrote the law and now lobby. They will serve as consultants for special interest groups that will stand to reap the rewards of public policy that was written for those who can afford to pay for an interpretation of the law. As lawmakers scurry to close loopholes hidden in policy, the ex-lawmakers who created those loopholes will exploit the loopholes to their fullest potential as well as lobby to keep them open. When these loopholes are created for foreign countries, the nation runs a particularly dangerous risk of subverting its interests by the very people who swore to uphold the nation's interest.

The danger posed by post-congressional retirement to US policy is hardly limited to the realm of foreign policy. Nor should the danger be limited to when former members of Congress become lobbyists. The former aides to members of Congress have been quite prevalent in the lobbying arena, so too have members of the executive branch and the federal bureaucracy. The danger posed to US policy is significant. When those entrusted to preserve and promote the public will compromise the public will for their own personal gain, the legitimacy and credibility of those institutions is undermined. When it happens with infrequency, the institutions are likely to recover with minimal damage. When it happens systematically, and with greater frequency, the difficulty with which the institutions recover grows considerably.

The legitimacy of democratic political institutions is of utmost importance, because it is in the legitimacy of the institutions that the power to govern resides. In democratic societies, the power ultimately rests in the people. And, in order for authoritative institutions to create policy deemed legitimate by the public, these institutions must maintain a certain level of support from the populace. William Gamson writes that when political institutions have high levels of public trust, "the authorities are able to make new commitments on the basis of it and, if successful, increase such support even more. When it is low or declining, authorities may find it difficult to meet existing commitments and govern effectively" (1968, 45-46). Arthur Miller further warns of the danger when he states, "A democratic political system cannot survive for long without the support of a majority of its citizens" (1974, 951). Symour Martin Lipset has found evidence to support the importance of legitimacy. Looking at the 1930s, when democratic regimes were under a multitude of pressures, those that induced a sense of trust, weathered the pressures of anti-democratic forces much more effectively, than those that had failed to do so (1960). My contention is that policy makers who leave their positions as policy makers to become lobbyists could compromise the legitimacy of American political institutions. The legitimacy of the US Congress is threatened by the practice of post-congressional lobbying. Pamela Gilbert of Congress Watch expresses this concern when she states that the issue of the revolving door "breeds public cynicism about government," and "It's very destructive to our political process" (Harbison 1993, A-3). As former members of Congress continue to return to the institution that they were once a part of as lobbyists we may well see a decline in support for the institution.

Two actors – individual citizens and the institutions create political legitimacy. Congress, by its actions produced its own sense of legitimacy from the populace. In order for this sense of legitimacy to exist Congress must offer reasons for the support, and it does so with its actions. When Congress expresses the will of the people in the policies that it creates, the populace in turn reciprocates Congress' gesture of sound policy with popular support. Stephen Weatherford identifies four characteristics of legitimate political institutions:

1. *Accountability.* Are rulers accountable to the governed via a process that allows wide, effective participation?
2. *Efficiency.* Is the government set up to accomplish society's ends without undue waste of time or resources?
3. *Procedural fairness.* Is the system structured to ensure that issues are resolved in a regular, predictable way and that access to decisional arenas is open and equal?
4. *Distributive fairness.* Are the advantages and costs allocated by the system distributed equally or else deviations from prima facie equality explicitly justified on grounds that define "fair shares" in terms of some long-run, overarching equality principles? (Weatherford 1992, 150).

How these questions are answered determines the extent to which the government is functioning in a manner that is in agreement with the populaces' preferences. The questions of *accountability* and *procedural fairness* focus on the process of governance. Is there a process for holding officials accountable, and does this process allow for the involvement of the public? Is there a way of resolving the issue in a *regular* and *predictable way*? Questions two and four, on the other hand, deal with the *goal* of government. In the *end*, is there undue waste of time and resources? And, is equality attained in the long run? The legitimacy of political institutions is in large part driven by whether the goals of society are achieved, and whether the process for achieving those goals is fair and effective.

According to the procedural criteria (items 1 and 3), an institution would be deemed legitimate if it allowed for methods of accountability through effective participation. But, because the population of members of Congress that we are analyzing in this text is precisely those who are retiring from Congress, the primary method for insuring effective participation – the electoral system – is mute. Conducting elections will not insure accountability. Those who are not seeking reelection, or who have lost their reelection bid are, from that point on, accountable to no one. It is particularly, among those who have voluntarily retired that pose the greatest danger. They are more likely to plan a strategy for exit that includes sponsoring legislation that benefits their future employers. Those who plan their exit from Congress are able to exploit their last term for their personal gain. Accountability through the electoral system only works when the member of Congress wants to continue in the position. As soon as the desire to remain in office is gone, the value of representation is diminished. Similarly, while *procedural fairness* is called for so that issues may be resolved in a regular and predictable manner, the "fairness" is comprised by the lack of accountability. If members of Congress are not obliged to do the bidding of their constituents because they will not seek reelection, then the process of resolving issues is compromised.

The substantive or, outcome criteria (items 2 and 4), is also compromised by an institution that rewards its members for leaving office to return as lobbyists. The institution can threaten its own legitimacy by passing legislation that is not the most efficient or fair in a distributive sense. If members of Congress sponsor legislation for their future employers, the outcome may not be in the best interest of the nation or even of the individual representative's constituents. It would be difficult to claim that the government is positioned to remedy societal ills without undue waste if legislators, especially retiring legislators, can sponsor and enact legislation that benefits a future employer at the expense of the interest of their constituents. The rule of efficiency is violated when resources are wasted. And resources would be wasted if the legislation rewarded interest groups with legislation that would increase costs to constituents. If an interest group were rewarded with a piece of legislation that keeps rivals out of the market place, then consumers would pay the cost in higher prices. In instances in which legislators are retiring, and thus no longer responsive to their constituents, those legislators may be more likely to sponsor unpopular legislation – legislation that could prove costly to consumers and voters.

The efficiency and distributional fairness criteria are further violated when ex-lawmakers leave office. As addressed earlier, ex-lawmaker lobbyists are given tremendous advantages over their non-ex-lawmaker lobbyist colleagues. Their access to current lawmakers gives them the opportunity to make their case to their old friends while those without the same familiar connections to current members of Congress are not given equal access. Friendship becomes more important than knowledge of public policy. This access based on friendship means not only that post-congressional lobbyists get access, but also they can take on more questionable clients and lobby for more unpopular interest. Pluralist theory tells us that group competition is fair because all groups have access to policy makers. No matter how small or large, how well funded or poorly funded, special interest groups have the right to petition the government. Those groups that hire former members of Congress as lobbyists have a greater advantage than groups that do not hire them – "It gives special access to some lobbying groups" (Harbison 1993, A-3). While the pluralist theory does not require that groups be equal, it does suggest that they have equal access to public officials. However, when those who are lobbying are those who have close and intimate relations with those who will be lobbied, then those lobbyists with the intimate relationships have an added advantage in the process of petitioning the government.

The evidence presented here is more likely to support the elite theory. Dye and Zeigler have suggested that it is the elites who set the political agenda (1996, 400). These policy elites do not overtly influence government. Rather, they select those who will be team players to promote the policy on their behalf. Dye and Zeigler state:

> Those at the top of influential structures need not exercise their power overtly; the subordinates who carry on the day-to day business of industry, finance, government, and the media know the values of their bosses. These subordinates obtained their jobs in part because they exhibited elite values in their thinking and actions. Whether consciously or unconsciously, their decisions reflect the values of those at the top (1996, 403).

Members of Congress who later go on to become lobbyists, one might speculate, are themselves political elites or are selected by political elites to continue to do their bidding. One finds that those ex-lawmakers who represent better educated and wealthier constituency are more likely to become lobbyists. The probability that an ex-lawmaker will become a lobbyist will increase by 23 percent as the level of education in the congressional district increases, and by 16 percent as the income level increases. Dye and Zeigler go on to suggest that representation is not the "will of the people", but rather, it is "at best"… "intraelite communication" (1996, 300). The same people who create the law lobby government on behalf of interests that are impacted by the law. Charles Lewis, Charles, Executive Director of the Center for Public Integrity agrees, stating:

> Things have gotten so incestuous inside Washington. There is a permanent ruling class, a permanent ruling elite that makes decisions affecting everyone. But the most elite are not elected. Officials are

> trading on their public positions and feathering their own nests. The lines become blurred between public and private (Borders and Dockery 1995, 15).

The "incestuous" relationship described by Charles Lewis, Charles is consistent with the elite theory, which suggests that a ruling class governs, as opposed to a series of groups as described by the pluralist theory.

Glenn Parker shows that the increase in rent-seeking opportunities, or the costs associated with extracting monopoly rights from Congress has had a negligible effect on legislative service (1996, 123). Members of Congress have become disillusioned with service because of their dependence on campaign contributors who in turn seek to extract certain concessions from government. The decline in legislative service has meant the shortening of congressional careers, and turning public service into methods of enhancing the legislators' own ambitions. Discrete ambition contributes to the decline in the accountability and fairness of the political process and outcome. It also leads to an increase in waste (Parker 1996). As the amount of rent-seeking continues to grow one also witnesses a decrease in the level of support given to Congress and individual members of Congress by the American people. Citing National Election Studies from 1968 to 1980 and Roper data, Parker shows that increasingly there is a public sense that legislators have little concern for voters, and that legislators are increasingly more concerned with their self-interest (Parker 1996, 72-73). The evidence further suggests that the decline in support for Congress has corresponded with the decentralization of Congress. As Congress has become more decentralized, its members have become more inclined to satisfy self-interests. And, as they become self-interested actors, the legitimacy of the institution has been undermined. Increasingly, more experienced members of Congress are choosing to leave Congress in part because they no longer see any intrinsic value in serving. Parker writes:

> When the job of the member of Congress, and the institution in which he or she serves, are viewed with public contempt, respected politicians will steer clear of the opportunity to serve. This is exactly the situation evolving in Congress: the intrinsic benefits are gradually disappearing as the public's negative view of members of Congress and Congress itself demeans and denigrates legislative service (1996, 68).

Parker goes on to say that as these trends continue, the ultimate goal of serving in Congress will be "financial gain obtained by serving as an intermediary in dealings between" interest groups and government (1996, 68). Just as campaign contributions are part of that financial gain, increasingly, so to are the lobbying opportunities for ex-lawmakers.

Time and time again, survey research has shown the American people's frustration with its political institutions and with Congress in particular. Congress itself has caused the decline in support for the institution. As Congress decentralized, its members have been afforded a great deal of autonomy in legislative activity with little supervision. The decline in the importance of the seniority rule, the deference to committees on policy matters, and the weakening of party leadership led to a loosening of the reigns on members of Congress. No matter how much recent Congressional leaders have attempted to reign in rank-and-file members of Congress, the lure of political autonomy has been too great for members of Congress to give up so readily. It has become increasingly difficult for lawmakers to bring sanctions against colleagues that may be undermining the public trust or the nations' laws. As members of Congress are granted greater liberty from partisan or institutional constraints, they are free to develop their own relationships with special interest groups. These relationships, as we are discovering, are increasingly extending to the life of the lawmakers well past their tenure as elected officials.

Well over two centuries ago, James Madison warned against the accumulation of power. He wrote in Federalist 47:

> The accumulation of all powers, legislative, executive, and judiciary, in the same hands, whether of one, a few, or many, and whether hereditary, self-appointed, or elective, may justly be pronounced the very definition of tyranny (Hamilton, Madison, Jay [1788] 1999, 269).

While Madison and the framers of the Constitution may very well have felt as though they had resolved the problem of tyranny with the separation of powers and the creation of the federalist system, we are increasingly moving in the direction of a political system in which power is no longer as separate as it may once have been. Increasingly we find members of Congress and their aides rotate out of the institution only to reappear in the guise of a member of the executive branch, or as a lobbyist. When the petitioner is a former legislator, the opportunity for mischief is heightened.

Conclusion

In this chapter, I have discussed some of the additional dangers of permitting ex-lawmakers to lobby government. When ex-lawmakers lobby, their former status as policy makers gives them tremendous advantages over other lobbyists. Ex-lawmakers are able to capitalize on their friendships with existing lawmakers whom they once worked with in Congress. Post-congressional lobbyists not only have these special friendships, they are also afforded special privileges as former lawmakers – to walk the chamber floor, use facilities specially earmarked for members of Congress etc. These special privileges and connections give members of Congress access to lawmakers that other lobbying groups do not have. As a consequence, the policy positions that ex-lawmakers endorse are given a better chance of becoming policy. Because of their status and because of their connections, they are given tremendous advantages over other lobbyists, and that in turn stifles competition. The danger in this is that the value of policy can be influenced greatly by the messenger rather than by the policy alone. While it would be naïve to assume that the worth of issues on which interest groups lobby is strictly determined by the issues alone, that the success of the issues be determined by the relationship that the lobbyist has with the lobbied is foolhardy and dangerous. When the value of an idea is determined in part by the fact that the person lobbying on behalf of an idea is a former member of Congress, the institution runs the danger of creating public policy that could prove harmful to the country.

Ex-lawmakers, knowing that they can capitalize on their friendships with current lawmakers, are becoming bolder about announcing their intentions to become lobbyists. This boldness raises questions about the integrity of policy supported by these ex-lawmakers-turned-lobbyists. It raises questions about what their true motivations may have been during their last term in office. It also raises questions about those left behind. Current lawmakers, witnessing the success of their former colleagues may themselves plan their own future as lobbyists. Among the dangers associated with post-congressional lobbying is that ex-lawmakers are better positioned to lobby on behalf of foreign interests, or on behalf of interests that are antithetical to American interests. In this chapter a few examples of ex-lawmakers lobbying on behalf of foreign governments or on behalf of businesses wanting to conduct trade with foreign governments were provided. That which makes ex-lawmakers such great lobbyists – their access to their former colleagues – is the very thing that makes ex-lawmakers valuable to special interests groups that may not be particularly popular in Washington. Some ex-lawmakers, because of their celebrity status in American government are able to lobby for some of the least popular interests. At stake is the legitimacy of the US Congress. The American people give Congress its ultimate power – its legitimacy. When those who compose the institution use the institution as training grounds for future employment, the American people take notice. And when the American people take notice, the institution suffers. Post-congressional lobbying undermines the criterion that tests for the legitimacy of political institutions. Post-congressional lobbying disparages, not only the institution but also its great works.

---

[1] See Lloyd Grove. 2003. "They're Nervous, but on the Surface They Look Calm and Ready", *Washington Post*, June 25 Page C03.

---

[2] He would later reveal that he represented Taiwanese interests when he appeared on the Larry King Show with his wife, Elizabeth (CNN Transcripts 2000).
[3] Loral Space and Communications is a satellite communications company.

7

Conclusion

Congress, by some standards, has been an institution in a constant state of change. Whether that change has been linear or circular, however, is still not altogether clear. Nelson Polsby (1968) has implied that the development of Congress has been linear, suggesting a gradual improvement in the institutionalization and professionalization of the institution. According to Polsby Congress has become more institutionalized (1968). To support the argument that Congress has become more institutionalized, he points to what might be perceives as the professionalization of congressional careers. Congressional careers have become longer, and this lengthening of careers serves to indicate that Congress has become more institutionalized. By Polsby's account, representatives go into Congress with the intent of holding office almost permanently. The reward for public service would be the power gained from service rather than some pecuniary benefit. The goal would be to represent the interests of the representatives' constituents as faithfully as possible.

But, if Congress has not become more institutionalized, then one might expect to see that pecuniary benefits remain important. One might also expect to see lawmakers come and go from Congress with greater frequency, and of their own volition. If Congress goes in and out of "institutionalization", then we would expect to see a diminution in the value of service. Under such conditions it would not be unusual to see ex-lawmakers leave public service to pursue a more lucrative career as lobbyists. If the seniority rule and the power associated with chairing a committee have disappeared, then we would expect a decline in the number of members who would want to serve longer periods. They would not wish to stay longer because they would not be rewarded for doing so.

Disputing the claim that Congress has become more institutionalized is Lawrence Dodd (1985), who argues that the development of Congress has been cyclical rather than linear. Thomas Cavanaugh similarly has concluded, "the politically salient characteristics of the House appear to be receding from the model of institutionalized House presented in Polsby's article" (1980, 637). Congress goes through phases where, at times, power is more centralized and at times it is decentralized. As power is decentralized – distributing it to the committees, and later to the individual members – Congress is weakened, making it vulnerable to other institutions, particularly the presidency. Congress then reacts to the presidency's gaining the advantage by centralizing power (Dodd 1985,500). If Congress goes through these phases, then we might expect these phases to be manifested in the reactions that members of Congress have toward the institution (see Frantzich 1978; Cooper and West 1981).

It might be the case that Polsby's position that Congress was becoming more institutionalized was due to measuring the development of the House and Senate as it was becoming more institutionalized – as power was becoming more centralized. By the early to mid 1970s members of Congress began to make greater demands for a more equal distribution of power in Congress. This was in large part due to the ideological homogenization of the dominant Democratic Party. If it was the case that Congress had become decentralized by the mid-1970s, then it was likely that Congress would be in a weakened position to offer legislators incentives to stay in office. The incentives to stay in office were undermined by two forces that were at their strongest during the Ninety-third Congress. The first of these was the challenge to the seniority rule, and the second was the equalization of power. The changes that ensued in these two areas made differentiation between experienced representatives and less experienced representatives almost obsolete (Hibbing 1982, 94)[1]. If the congressional changes had an impact on the desirability of serving in Congress, then we should see a change in service after 1976. Those who retired before 1976 would have served when it was still "fun" to serve. They would have been less likely to pursue post-congressional employment, because they would have been at retirement age when they left Congress. Those who retired before 1976 and had not been in Congress very long would not have been very appealing to interest groups in need of a lobbyist. Milbrath reported that lobbying organizations were reluctant to hire former members of Congress during the 1960s. He reasoned, "The defeated member is probably not strikingly capable; also, he is unlikely to have the technical skills and knowledge that many lobby jobs require" (1963,68).

Those who retired after 1976, on the other hand, may have served shorter periods, and would have been more likely to stay in Washington upon retirement. They would have retired in Washington because the changes in Congress, which brought an equalization of power to more members, suddenly brought less seasoned representatives in close contact with interest groups. Interest groups, recognizing that even freshman representatives had some power to influence legislation, would have been inclined to lobby rank-and-file members of Congress. This contact contributed to the reinforcement of iron triangles in which representatives formed relationships with interest groups and bureaucrats (see Freeman 1965). These two factors – the decline in the seniority rule and the equalization of power – arguably have begun to undercut the institutionalization of Congress. With the decline in importance of the seniority rule and the equalization of power among members of Congress, one began to see a decline in the importance of a long congressional career on the part of members of Congress. Hibbing cites two members of Congress who retired in 1978:

> In the old days, a member with 8 or 10 years of service was very reluctant to retire because he was throwing away years of stored capital, dues paying or whatever you want to call it. Now 8 or 10 years means nothing. You're not giving up much by retiring because you might have been denied your chair even if you had seniority. Why stay? (1982,94).

> Most members these days have as much power in their second term as they will in their eight, so what is there to look forward to? (1982,94).

If members give less value to congressional careers because of the decline in incentives, then they may be more likely to retire early. If they are more likely to retire early, then they will be more likely to attempt to profit from their congressional experience. And if they are more likely to profit from their congressional experience, they will be more likely to retire to become lobbyists.

What we find is that the increase in post-congressional lobbying has coincided since the de-institutionalization of Congress. Of those who left office before the congressional changes of the early 1970s only about 6 percent would become lobbyists. Post-1975, 33 percent of the ex-lawmakers would find themselves as registered lobbyists. The de-institutionalization of Congress contributed heavily to a culture that permitted self-serving, autonomous behavior. And, while in recent years, political parties have attempted to reign in the rank-and-file members, all too often, the parties are willing to compromise with the rank-and-file on what the party deems minor points for political support on major policy questions. What might seem a minor policy point may be a major concession to a special interest group.

It is not as though Congress has not had the opportunity to improve its condition. The opportunity presented itself in the early 1990s when the Republicans took control of Congress, but rather than strengthen the leadership, it opted to weaken the institution, by weakening the power of the Speaker and limiting the terms served by committee chairs. Such moves, rather than strengthening the power of Congress, have only served to weaken it. Prior to the Republican takeover of Congress, the Republicans, under the leadership of Newt

Gingrich were quite successful at inculcating the message in the American people that Congress, and particularly the Democrats who controlled Congress had failed to adequately serve the American people. The claim was that Congress, under Democratic rule, was too beholden to special interest groups, and was overspending public funds to accommodate the interests of these groups. Republicans had successfully attacked the Democrats for their willingness to perpetuate what Theodore Lowi calls "interest group liberalism". The nation's deficit and debt were both soaring out of control, and this was in part blamed on Congress' inability to deny the wishes of special interest groups.

Having had the opportunity to strengthen Congress under new leadership, the Republicans opted to weaken the institution. On the surface this seemingly makes no sense. Asks Lawrence Dodd:

> Why, at their moment of victory, did the Republicans not follow through and implement real reform, choosing instead to undercut the very centralized leadership that had "brought them to the dance"? Why did they maneuver, moreover, for constitutional changes such as term limits and budget constraints that would seem to limit their own power as majority party? Why did the Republicans themselves so rapidly become the object of public scorn? And why did factional problems emerge so rapidly at the highest levels of leadership activity, so that the Republicans' governing capacities were thrown into serious question despite their great electoral victory (2005, 421)?

Why these actions were taken when they would obviously undermine the legitimacy of the institution is an enigma. Part of the answer to these questions rests on the difficulty the institution faces in shifting from being a product of an industrial society to being a product of the post-industrial society (Dodd 2005, 423). But part of the explanation may also rest on the need to further undermine the institution before it can be repaired. By allowing the popular sentiment of the institution to get so low that the public will demand a revamping of the institution might be the only way to redesign the institution for the post-industrial era. While it has not been made entirely clear what the new design might be, there have been boasts on the part of some to reduce the size of government to where it can be drowned "in the bathtub" (Norquist 2001). Dodd predicts,

> Although the severity of public hostilities will vary with the boom and bust cycles of national economies, declining somewhat in good times, the public's growing disenchantment with governing institutions eventually should produce a breakdown in democratic government (2005, 424).

Such ominous predictions highlight the possibility that the future of American government is that of a collection of weak institutions that are far less obtrusive than current governmental institutions.

Furthering the cause of "un-popularizing" popular government is the unregulated permissive behavior of current and former members of Congress. As lawmakers continue to "run against" Congress in their own elections they continue to promote the sentiment that what Congress does is somehow bad. It is Congress that is misspending tax dollars. It is Congress that is over-regulating the lives of every American. It is Congress that creates public policy that grows the government. As members of Congress return to their districts to run for re-election they increasingly run against Congress rather than against challengers. Running against Congress is becoming an even more popular sport for members of Congress because increasingly, congressional district lines are being drawn so as to elect incumbents or members of a particular party. Cutting down on electoral competition forces members of Congress to run against the very institution to which they belong. In doing so, Congress suffers the public's unpopular blows.

Further contributing to the disparagement of Congress is the rude, and, at times, unethical behavior of members of Congress. While Congress has always had more than its share of scandals, now, more than ever, the public can be informed of much mischief considerably sooner and more pervasively than ever before. Allegations of unethical behavior on the part of high-ranking lawmakers like Speakers Jim Wright and Newt Gingrich raise questions of their integrity as well as that of the institution they lead. The Abscam scandal of the 1970s, the pervasive check-writing scandal of the 1990s, and many other minor scandals and lapses in judgment have contributed to the diminution of respect granted to Congress by the American people. Some of the lowest levels of support for the US Congress in recent times have been precisely during these scandals, while the highest levels of support for the US Congress has been immediately after the September 11th tragedy of 2001. But rather than capitalize on the positive sentiments that the American people expressed toward Congress, it quickly reverted to the partisan acrimony that has been the hallmark of recent Congresses. Opportunities to improve the image of Congress have rather carelessly been squandered in favor of the status quo. Whether intentional or unintentional, Congress loses integrity when it takes actions deemed unsavory by the public.

The practice of post-congressional lobbying is of this kind of behavior that compromises the integrity of the institution. In general, the public is not surprised that many former members of Congress become lobbyists. The public seems to expect ex-lawmakers to exploit their congressional careers in this fashion. But, while the public expects it, it does not appreciate it. During the writing of this book, I had an opportunity to speak with many Americans about this project. Repeatedly, individuals expressed the sentiment that they expect their public officials to ingratiate themselves to lobbying groups and special interest groups upon leaving office. While the public often times expects questionable behavior from public officials, they have no appreciation for it. The public, all too often, turns those sentiments into negative attitudes toward the institution itself.

Some Solutions

The problems with post-congressional lobbying can be summarized into two major problems. The first of these is the problem that lawmakers planning to become lobbyists could create public policy to benefit their future employers. The second is that ex-lawmakers are able to capitalize on their relationship with former colleagues, thus providing the groups that they lobby for added advantage. How to minimize or prevent these two problems is the purpose of this final chapter. The solution to both of these problems is simple – prevent ex-lawmakers from ever lobbying. I propose several ways in which post-congressional lobbying can be prevented without creating excessive regulations, or being onerous on ex-lawmakers. There are three predominant actors in post-congressional lobbying – the ex-lawmakers themselves, the existing lawmakers, and the special interest groups that hire ex-lawmakers. In this chapter I will discuss ways in which the behavior of these three groups of actors can be controlled.

In this study we have found that a significant number of members of Congress retire to become lobbyists. We have further found that this practice of lobbying has implications for public policy and the sponsoring of new legislation. The post-congressional career choice of many former members of Congress may further contribute to the decay in the legitimacy of Congress. As more public officials choose to profit from their congressional careers, public sentiment toward the institution may be expected to decline further. To resolve the problem caused by the profiting from a post-congressional career at the public's expense, many have suggested the imposition of term limits. Term limits would require members of Congress to leave their posts after as certain number of terms. This, however, would only have the effect of creating a greater number of former members of Congress who would become lobbyists. If former members were required to retire after a certain amount of time in office, many would be forced from office at a time in their life when they would have to find remunerative work. Ex-lawmakers would likely decide to use their newly created expertise and experience to work as lobbyists, thus exacerbating the problem of post-congressional lobbying.

Regulating post-congressional lobbying by outlawing lobbying for a short period of time also has a negligible impact on lobbying. As we are finding, a one-year ban on post-congressional lobbying does little to keep ex-lawmakers from lobbying[2]. Former member of Congress Bill Gradison once said, "For a while I carried the statute in my pocket, in fact, I think I still have it here". He continues:

> I took it and put some plastic on either side and carried it around. I memorized the phrase: We're not permitted to contact a member of the House or Senate or their staff, quote, 'with the intent to influence official action,' closed quote. I remember that, and I don't think there were any close calls. I bent over backwards to avoid anything that might even look inappropriate (Borders and Dockery 1995, 19).

Gradison, like many others, waited out the one-year ban, and now is lobbying successfully in Congress. Ex-lawmakers are wasting no time to become consultants for major lobbying firms. On the payroll, these ex-lawmakers can wait out the one-year ban, providing advise to the firms that hire them on how best to approach certain members of Congress. Once the first year is over ex-lawmakers are not restricted from contacting their former colleagues. A permanent ban would be in order, however, there are ways of preventing post-congressional lobbying without creating legislation, which in the end can be circumvented by clever individuals.

One solution to preventing ex-lawmakers form lobbying is to encourage them to continue to serve. Rather than reducing the length of congressional service so as to punish those that are reelected by their constituents, Congress, as an institution would be better served if the length of service were extended. While there are exceptions, ex-lawmakers who serve well into old age are less likely to seek post-congressional lobbying careers. Clearly, some might express concern that members of Congress who serve long tenures tend to lose touch with their constituents; the electoral system will take care to prevent that from occurring. Lott and Davis have concluded that elections do allow for the removal from office those who shirk or deviate from the views of their constituents (1992, 470). Lott and Reed take the argument further, suggesting that the length of terms in office and the congruence between voters and their representatives may be high. The reason for the greater congruence is because voters have been given the opportunity to remove those officials whose policy preferences do not correspond with theirs (Lott and Reed 1989). These studies suggest that the electoral process functions properly, allowing those whose views do not fit together with their constituents, to be voted out of office. This is precisely how the system was intended to work.

How can ex-lawmakers be encouraged to continue to serve? Congress might begin by reinstating the seniority rule. Rank-and-file members of Congress can be encouraged to continue to serve if they are rewarded for doing so. Serving as chair of a congressional committee is not only an honor, but it also provides the chair a great deal of power. Members who have served for long periods of time should be rewarded with such authority. All too frequently, the modern Congress makes virtually no distinction between a representative who has only served two terms and one who has served ten terms (Hibbing 1982, 94). As the line is blurred between junior and senior lawmakers, the value of the office is diminished.

By making congressional service a more rewarding experience, where long tenures lead to greater power and prestige, we should see a professionalization of Congress. By re-instituting the seniority rule, serving in Congress can be made "fun again". Parker suggests that those who serve because they receive some intrinsic returns from doing so need to be rewarded so that they may remain in office. While many have pointed to the problems caused by the seniority rule, such as giving greater power to certain regions or certain age groups, it nevertheless allows for a more objective manner of selecting chairs. Selecting leaders through the use of the seniority rule insures that it is the experienced politicians who will head the committees. And, because a rule is used in the selection of the committees rather than fellow members or leaders, it insures that egos are not hurt – producing a "more cooperative atmosphere" (Parker 1996, 142).

There are several other possible solutions to the problem of post-congressional lobbying that involve institutional changes. Since a fair number of congress members-turned-lobbyists tend to come from the powerful committees such as Ways and Means and Appropriations, it might serve a useful purpose to weaken the powers of the members of those committees. By making it more difficult for these individuals to sponsor legislation for interest groups that may employ them later, they will not be as valuable to the special interests as they are currently. Cutting down on the practice of multiple referrals may achieve this goal. By eliminating the referral of a bill to one of the powerful committees, or their subcommittees, then one can eliminate the role played by the Ways and Means, Appropriations, Budget, and Rules Committees. This in turn would make the individual members of these committees less valuable to special interests.

Not all solutions to the problem of post-congressional lobbying require that congressional rules be changed. While passing laws stating that members must refrain from lobbying for a period of time could be a solution, perhaps a better enticement would be to make the members of Congress dependent on their constituents for their housing. Many members of Congress end up having to purchase homes in Washington DC. This could conceivably make remaining in the Washington DC area more likely. As a solution to the problem of having so many ex-members of Congress remaining in Washington DC after their congressional service is over, one might consider state funded housing while the member is in service. The various state governments may consider purchasing or building homes in the Washington area for the members of their congressional delegations. These homes would remove much of the financial burden which members often times have to contend with when serving in Congress. State funded private residences may also attract more qualified candidates since those with modest means may currently be reluctant to run for office because of the financial burden of owning two homes[3]. Once the members of Congress vacate their posts they would be required to vacate their homes, which would be the property of the respective states. Just as a former president is required to vacate the White House for the incoming president, so to would the retiring members of Congress. As a consequence, one might expect that these individuals would find it particularly difficult to remain in Washington DC. And since they would not have been financially burdened with the purchase of a second home, many might choose not to sell their homes in their home district. Once they left office, they would return to their homes in their home states.

Finally, the American people need to be given a reason to revere the US Congress. During the Watergate hearings the American people saw the US Congress at its best, ensuring that the political process was not undermined by the ambitions of a few. The Watergate hearings brought to light, not only the great dangers of power gone unchecked, but also the capacity of one institution to check the other. It is when Congress works for the benefit of the common good that the institution's legitimacy increases. In keeping a check on the powers of the president, Congress performs just such a function and as such would be revered, if only for a moment, by the American People. Congress can regain its legitimacy if it can convince the American people that its members are concerned, not with personal economic gain, but with the creation of public policy that is in the interest of the constituents.

Bureaucrats, Aides, and Sister too

This book has focused exclusively on members of Congress and ex-lawmakers of Congress. It would be a mistake to assume that the revolving-door problem is limited to former members of Congress. Directories of registered lobbyists list a significant number of former generals, admirals and other military officials who have crossed over to the public sector becoming highly paid lobbyists for industries that produce weapons. Former military officials bring with them a significant amount of credibility. Many of these individuals have worked closely with those industries that produce weapons for years. Many have developed a tremendous amount of expertise about the weapons, and the companies that make those weapons. These former military officials take this knowledge and then go to lobby for those weapons systems and the companies that make those weapons. They also develop a tremendous amount of expertise about how the government decides which weapons it will purchase. And of course, like ex-lawmakers, they have access to their former colleagues. While there are restrictions on lobbying immediately after leaving a post, nothing prevents these individuals from sharing their knowledge so as to win lucrative contracts for the corporations that employ them. While no one is suggesting that it is wrong to use the knowledge gained from public service to make a profit, what is a problem is when that knowledge is used to lobby for and create public policy that is not in the interest of the American people.

Aides to members of Congress are also notorious for pursuing lobbying careers after serving a few years. The aides to lawmakers who served on powerful committees can develop expertise on the policy issues that those committees oversaw. This expertise, coupled with the connections to their former bosses who may still be in office, make them valuable lobbyists for special interest groups. Some of these aides can earn million dollar contracts as lobbyists. Some of these former aides can earn lucrative salaries by lobbying a single committee or a single member of Congress. Jill Abramson reports on one such aide.

> Boutique firms that specialize in lobbying a single member or a single committee of Congress have also sprouted up and are flourishing. Ann M. Eppard, who for 22 years served as a top aide to Bud Shuster, the House Transportation Committee chairman, left her job in 1994 and hung out her shingle as a transportation lobbyist. Within months, she had lined up more than $1 million in retainers from an array of big transportation companies, including the FDX Corporation (Abramson 1998, A1).

The success that such aides have as lobbyists is sending signals to other aides that the next step in their congressional careers as aides is lobbying. It is in lobbying that aides can dramatically improve their economic fortunes.

All too often, the family members of prominent lawmakers take on the role of lobbyists. The brothers and sisters, sons and daughters, husbands and wives of many prominent lawmakers have become lobbyists, gaining access to other lawmakers in the process. Here too there is danger. It is conceivable that lawmakers might share information with their family members that will give them an advantage when lobbying on behalf of some special interest group. Here the danger is that the public trust can be compromised. In some instances the lawmakers themselves benefit from the success of their family members' success in lobbying their colleagues. If the family member is successful in lobbying for a particular issue, that family member may be paid a better salary, attract other clients, or establish their own lobbying firm that the lawmaker can then move into when out of office. If lawmakers see their economic fortunes connected to the economic fortunes of their spouses, siblings, or offspring, they may be tempted to purse the lobbyist family member's agenda. Sound policy may be compromised for questionable policy when the fortunes of lawmakers are so intrinsically tied to the lobbying successes of their family members.

Summary

The framers of the Constitution understood that in order to obtain good governance from a republican government, political institutions would have to be made up of ambitious individuals who would be willing to compete with some frequency to hold on to their positions of power. Elections in America do that rather effectively. Granted that congressional elections tend to give incumbents an advantage, elections have tended to insure that members of Congress do not shirk too far from the preferred policy position of their constituents' preferences. Ambition has attracted a steadily improving quality of elected officials. Now more than ever, elected officials are well educated and experienced in policy making. Many members of Congress have life histories that indicate their legislative prowess and capacity for negotiation. With little reservation, the US Congress attracts the best and the brightest. These are individuals who have a far greater sense of civic duty than most Americans. They sacrifice personal wealth for the purpose of serving their country and their fellow Americans.

While the US Congress attracts such high quality individuals, the framers of the Constitution understood that it would be unwise to rely on the caliber of the individual alone to determine who gets to serve in public office and who does not. The framers of the Constitution wrote a document that protects the American people from the avarice and ambition of individuals that might not have the best interest of the American people at heart. Elections would be the primary mechanism for providing this protection. But what the framers did not provide meaningful protections from was the ambition of members of Congress who opted to return to private life. For those who chose not to continue to serve, the only watchdog protecting Americans from their discrete ambitions have been other members of Congress. Exiting lawmakers, who may attempt to exploit their position to enact legislation that may reward their future employers are generally thwarted from such action by their fellow colleagues who have obligations to their constituents to create sound public policy. While this protection generally works very well, experienced lawmakers can navigate through the complex process of policy making. Exiting members of Congress are sufficiently skilled at maneuvering bills through Congress. The temptation to shirk one's responsibility as a lawmaker is aggravated by the proliferation of interest groups in the 20th Century. As the lobbying industry grew during the latter half of the 20th Century, coupled with the decentralization of power in Congress, and a growing need for lawmakers to raise campaign funds, the stage was set for ex-lawmakers to make their move from Congress to K Street.

Both the lobbying industry and former members of Congress would benefit from the transformation of the member of the Congress from representative to lobbyist. The ex-lawmaker would bring significant expertise in policy, as well as congenial relations with existing lawmakers who would be able to help a former colleague get a bill through Congress. The Congresses of the 20th Century produced increasingly complex public policy, which in turn has produced an industry of policy experts just to understand the meaning, implementation and implications of public policy. One might imagine the lobbying industry asking itself, "Who would understand public policy better, than the creators of the policy?" Policy and procedural expertise, combined with strong connections to other members of Congress would be a major asset to any special interest group and lobbying firm. The members of Congress in turn, would benefit from post-congressional lobbying careers in several ways. By some accounts, the lawmaker would experience an increase in pay with a decrease in workload. The lawmaker would also avoid the difficult and time-consuming task of raising campaign funds and running for office.

The practice of post-congressional lobbying poses several serious dilemmas. First of all, the possibility that a former member of Congress might use the authority of the position to create policy that benefits the representative's future employer is perhaps the most serious consequence of post-congressional lobbying. In this book, it has been shown that members of Congress who become lobbyists do behave differently during their last term in office than those members who do not become lobbyists. It has been shown that those who become lobbyists remain legislatively more active than their non-lobbying colleagues from one Congress to the next. This difference suggests that lawmakers who are going to become lobbyists may be planning to become lobbyists, and so they are augmenting their behavior accordingly. One possibility that was discussed is that lawmakers who eventually become lobbyists are sending signals to potential employers. They may be sending the message that they are becoming available with the hopes that the lobbying industry might take notice of their policy expertise. What is reported in this book is that the actions of retiring members of Congress who become lobbyists may very well go beyond sending signals. Post-congressional lobbyists actually take action to help bills become law. So, while some signaling may be occurring, so to is rewarding. This book provides numerous examples of lawmakers who used their position to enact legislation that benefited specific groups. These same lawmakers would then leave office only to become employed by the very group that they sponsored legislation for.

While it is suggested that policy expertise is a significant factor in determining the value of a lobbyist, just as valuable is access to members of Congress. Post-congressional lobbyists are most valuable for their ability to gain access to their old friends. Access to powerful members of Congress is a valuable commodity that lobbying firms and special interest groups are willing to pay a hefty price for. Some lawmakers become celebrities, and celebrity status further opens doors to the offices of members of Congress. Celebrity ex-lawmakers, statesmen and stateswomen are afforded a significant amount of deference by their former colleagues on national and international questions. There is a danger in these revered ex-lawmakers being deferred to by existing lawmakers because the interests of post-congressional lobbyists may no longer be the interests of the nation.

Conclusion

With the growth of the lobbying industry in American government, the impact that the congressional revolving door is having on US public policy needs to be further evaluated. While the evidence was a mixture of qualitative and quantitative data, the evidence suggests that the revolving door is having a negligible impact on public policy. Further and more systematic research needs to be conducted to gauge the full impact of post-congressional lobbying on both public policy and the legitimacy of political institutions. Research on the efficiency and effectiveness of public policy created or lobbied for by post-congressional lobbyists would be a worthwhile venture. So too would an analysis of the lobbying activities of congressional aides, the family members of members of Congress, as well as members of the executive branch. Cross-state and cross-national comparisons of lobbying activity on the part of former public officials might also merit further investigations. This project opens opportunities for further research in many areas. These areas of research are just valuable both for the theoretical queries that they entertain, but also for the practical dimension of improving   governance.

---

[1] As power was dispensed to more representatives, lobbyists had more opportunities to influence government. And as power was dispensed to more representatives the control of the rank-and-file became less manageable. Post institutionalization representatives were less inclined to stay in office because of the decline in incentives. Before the 1970s, the committee chair had the most to lose if he or she lost the chair. The Chairpersons were already the careerists of Congress. They were the least inclined to compromise those positions. But as the power was increasingly shared, so that even the newer members received it, then the power of staying in office diminished. As newer members were assigned sub-committee and committee chairs, then this brought them closer and closer to interest groups which they regulated through their committees. Later we will discuss how the de-institutionalization of Congress has contributed to the undermining of legislative authority, and the creation of a Congress that serves as a stepping stone to a more profitable post congressional career. For now it is only safe to hypothesize that if Congress has developed in the cyclical manner that Dodd mentions, then we should expect that after 1976 members of Congress have been more likely to retire to DC than before.

[2] It is likely that the one-year ban is not sufficient to thwart lobbying activity on the part of former members. Perhaps a longer ban would be better at curbing such activity. Senator Feingold has attempted to raise the ban to two years, but at the request of Senator Connie Mack of Florida and chairman of the Legislative Branch Appropriations Subcommittee, the amendment would be adopted by voice vote, thus avoiding a recorded

vote. Connie Mack's maneuver made it easier to drop the amendment in conference, which it did. An extension on the lobbying ban might help reduce the number of former members who attempt to become lobbyists upon retiring.

[3] These state-funded homes should be attractive enough that members would be more inclined to live in them than in those that the members purchase themselves.

References

Abramson, Jill. "The Business of Persuasion Thrives in Nation's Capital." *The New York Times*, 28 September 1998, A01.

Abramson, Paul R., John H. Aldrich, and David W. Rohde. 1987. "Progressive Ambition among the United States Senators: 1972-1988." *Journal of Politics* 74 (1): 3-35.

Santos, Adolfo. 2003. "Post-Congressional Lobbying and Legislative Sponsorship: Do Members of Congress Reward Their Future Employers?" *LBJ Journal of Public Affairs* 16 (1): 56-64.

Santos, Adolfo. 2004. "The Role of Lobbying on Legislative Activity When Lawmakers Plan to Leave." *International Social Science Review* 79 (1 and 2): 44-55.

Advantage Associates. 2004. *Advantage Associates, Inc*. http://www.advantage-dc.com/ouradvantage.htm (December 9, 2004)

Alpert, Bruce and Bill Walsh. "On the Hill: News from the Louisiana Delegation in the Nation's Capital." *Times-Picayune*, February 15 2004, 9.

American Society of Association Executives. 1996. *Association in a Nut-shell*. Washington, DC: Americans Society of Association Executives.

Armey, Richard K. 2003. "The US Homeland Security Market: Complex Challenges, Unrivaled Partnership Opportunities." *Israel Venture Capital Journal*, (June 12) 2-3. www.ivc-online.com. (May 5, 2005).

Barone, Michael, Grant Ujifusa, Richard E. Cohen. 1995. *The Almanac of American Politics 1996.* Washington DC: National Journal.

Barone, Michael, Grant Ujifusa, Richard E. Cohen. 1997. *The Almanac of American Politics 1998.* Washington DC: National Journal.

Barone, Michael. 1990. *Our Country: The Shaping of America from Roosevelt to Reagan.* New York: Free Press.

Baumgartner, Frank R. and Beth L. Leech. 1998. *Basic Interests: the Importance of Groups in Politics and in Political Science.* Princeton, NJ: Princeton University Press.

Benenson, Bob. 1993. "Cuts in Subsidy Programs Rattle Farm Coalition." *Congressional Quarterly Weekly Report* 51 (October 23): 2884.

Berry, Jeffrey M. 1977. *Lobbying for the People: the Political Behavior of Public Interest Groups.* Princeton, NJ: Princeton University Press.

Berry, Jeffrey M. 1989. "Subgovernments, Issue Networks, and Political Conflict." In *Remaking American Politics,* ed. Richard Harris and Sidney Milkis. Boulder, CO: Westview Press.

Birnbaum, Jeffrey H. 1992. *The Lobbyists: How Influence Peddlers Get their Way in Washington.* New York: Times Books.

Birnbaum, Jeffrey H. "Lawmaker-Turned-Lobbyist A Growing Trend on the Hill." *Washington Post,* 20 June 2004, A 1.

Boller, Paul F. 1991. *Congressional Anecdotes.* New York: Oxford University Press.

Borders, Rebecca and C.C. Dockery. 1995. *Beyond the Hill: A Directory of Congress from 1984 to 1993 Where Have All the Members Gone?* Lanham MD: University Press of America.

Brace, Paul. 1984. "Progressive Ambition in the House: A Probabilistic Approach." *The Journal of Politics* 46 (2): 556-571.

Braun, Gerry. "Former Congressman Bates Tanned and Rested, but is He Ready?" *The San Diego Union-Tribune,* 6 March 1994, A3.

Brogan, Pamela. 1992. *The Torturers' Lobby: How Human Rights Abusing Nations Are Represented in Washington.* Washington DC: The Center for Public Integrity.

Brookshire, Robert G. and Dean F. Duncan III. 1983. "Congressional Career Patterns and Party Systems." *Legislative Studies Quarterly* 8 (1): 65-78.

Brown, Deward Clayton. 1980. *Electricity for Rural America*. Westport, CT: Greenwood Press.

Bullock, Charles S. III and Burdett A. Loomis. 1985. "The Changing Congressional Career." In *Congress Reconsidered*, 3rd ed. Ed Lawrence C. Dodd and Bruce I. Oppenheimer. Washington: Congressional Quarterly.

Burke, Edmund. 1770 [1999]. "Thoughts on the Cause of the Present Discontent" in *Select Works of Edmund Burke*. Payne Ed. Vol. 1. Indianapolis: Liberty Fund.

Burke, Edmund. 1790 [1950]. *Reflections on the Revolution in France*. London: Oxford University Press.

Burke, Edmund. 1791 [1962]. *Appeal from the New to the Old Whigs*. Indianapolis: Bobbs-Merrill.

Bush, George W. 2003. "President Signs Medicare Legislation: Remarks by the President at Signing of the Medicare Prescription Drug, Improvement and Modernization Act of 2003 DAR Constitution Hall." Office of the Press Secretary, December 8, http://www.whitehouse.gov/news/ releases/2003/12/ 20031208-2.html. (July 13, 2004).

Carey, John. 2001. "Philip Morris' Latest Smoke Screen." *Business Week*, 3741 (July 16): 43.

Carr, Rebecca. 1996. "Panel Shuts 'Revolving Door' When it Comes From Prison: Convicted Ex-Officials Could not Lobby; Work For Foreign Governments Limited." *Congressional Quarterly* 54 (June 1): 1517.

Carroll, James R. 2004. "Far from 1998." *The Courier-Journal*. http://www.courier-journal.com/localnews/2004/10/10ky/B2notebook 1010-6623.html. (November 9, 2004).

Cater, Douglass. 1964. *Power in Washington*. New York: Random House.

Cavanaugh, Thomas E. 1980. "The Dispersion of Authority in the House of Representatives." *Political Science Quarterly*, 97 (4): 623-37.

Center for Education Reform. 2004. "Charter Connection." *Press Release* May 5 http://www.edreform.com/index.cfm?fuseAction=document&document ID=176 0&sectionID=34&NEWSYEAR=2004. (July 17, 2004).

Center for Public Integrity. 1997a. "Bill Frenzel President-Ripon Society Former US Representative (R-Minnesota) Interviewed by Jeff Shear June 19, 1997." http://www.publicintegrity.org/dtaweb/BOC_T_BF.asp

?L1=20&L2=26&L3=10&L4=17&L5=0&State=   (November   21, 2004).

Center for Public Integrity. 1997b. "Thomas Hale Boggs Jr. Partner, Patton-Boggs Interviewed by Chuck Lewis August 15, 1997." http://www.publicintegrity.org/dtaweb/BOC_T_THB.asp?L1=20&L2= 26&L3=10&L4=12&L5=0&State= (November 21, 2004).

Center for Public Integrity. 1998. "David Kessler Former Commissioner, Food and Drug Administration Interviewed by Charles Lewis February 2, 1998." http://www.publicintegrity.org/dtaweb/BOC_T_DK.asp?L1=20 &L2=26&L3=10&L4=22&L5=0&State= (November 10, 2004).

Center for Responsive Politics. 1999. "Business-Labor-Ideology Split in Donations to Candidates." http://www.opensecrets.org/pubs/bigpicture 2000/bli/bli_all.Ihtml. (January 4, 2000).

Center for Responsive Politics. 2001. "2000 Election Overview: Stats at a Glance." http://www.opensecrets.org/2000elect/storysofar/index.asp. (January 10, 2004).

Center for Responsive Politics. 2004a. "Donor Lookup: Find Individual and Soft Money Contributors." http://www.opensecrets.org/indivs/index.asp. (July 23, 2004).

Center for Responsive Politics. 2004b. "Tobacco: Top 20 Senators." http://www.opensecrets.org/industries/recips.asp?Ind=A02&Cycle=199 8&recipdetail=S&Mem=Y&sortorder=U (November 9, 2004)

Center for Responsive Politics. 2004c. "Pro-Israel: Long Term Contribution Trends." http://www.opensecrets.org/Lobbyists/indusclient.asp?code= Q05&year=2000&txtSort=C (December 20, 2004).

Charter School Development Corporation. 2002. "About CSDC." http://www.csdc.org/about/. (July 19, 2004).

Clinton, William J. 1998. "Remarks in a roundtable discussion on tobacco in Carrollton, Kentucky." *Weekly Compilation of Presidential Documents*, vol. 34 issue 15. April 9, 1998. http://web32.epnet.com/citation.asp?tb= 1&_ug=sid+154E9A03%2D880A%2D40F1%2DAD76%2DA79EB51 1D14B%40sessionmgr4+dbs+aph+cp+1+2707&_us=hd+False+hs+Tru e+cst+0%3B2+or+Date+fh+False+ss+SO+sm+ES+sl+0+dstb+ES+ri+ KAAACB3C00000261+A99E&_uso=hd+False+tg%5B2+%2DTX+tg %5B1+%2DTX+tg%5B0+%2DTX+st%5B2+%2DBuyout+st%5B1+% 2DTobacco+st%5B0+%2DWendell++Ford+db%5B0+%2Daph+op%5

B2+%2DAnd+op%5B1+%2DAnd+op%5B0+%2D+44B9&fn=1&rn=1 (November 10, 2004).

CNN Transcripts. 2000. "Bob and Elizabeth Dole Discuss the State of American Politics." *Larry King Live,* Aired January 7th, 2000. http://edition. cnn.com/TRANSCRIPTS/0001/07/lkl.00.html. (December 13, 2004).

Colgate, Gregory. 1984. *National Trade and Professional Association of the United States 1982.* Washington DC: Columbia Books.

Congressional Quarterly Weekly Report. 1993. "Bill on REA Changes Wins Panel's OK." *Congressional Quarterly Weekly Report.* 51 (September 25): 2549.

Congressional Quarterly. *1957.* "361 Lobbyists Register, 12-year Total Is 4,775." *Congressional Quarterly Almanac.* 13: 739.

Congressional Quarterly. 1994. *Congressional Quarterly's Guide to US Elections:* 3rd edition. Washington DC: Congressional Quarterly Inc.

Cooper, Joseph and William West. 1981. "The Congressional Career in the 1970s." In *Congress Reconsidered.* 2nd ea., ed. Lawrence C. Dodd and Bruce I. Oppenheimer. Washington DC: Congressional Quarterly.

Daly, John. 1997. "Global Connections: Political Giving in the 1996 Elections by Foreign Agent and US Subsidiaries of Foreign Companies." *Center for Responsive Politics,* May 1997 http://www.opensecrets.org/pubs /global/global5.htm.(December 20, 2004)

Davidson, Roger H. and Walter J. Oleszek. 1994. *Congress and Its Members.* 4th ed. Washington DC: CQ Press.

Dawson and Associates, Inc. 2004. *Dawson and Associates, Inc.* http://www.dawsonassociates.com. (July 22, 2004).

Department of Justice. 2004. "FARA Q and A." http://www.usdoj.gov/ criminal/fara/q_A.htm. (November 26, 2004).

Dodd, Lawrence C. 1985. "Congress and the Quest for Power." In *Studies of Congress,* ed. Glenn R. Parker. Washington DC: Congressional Quarterly.

Dodd, Lawrence C. 2005. "Re-Envisioning Congress: Theoretical Perspectives on Congressional Change – 2004." *Congress Reconsidered,* Washington DC: Congressional Quarterly.

Downs, Anthony. 1957. *An Economic Theory of Democracy.* New York: Harper and Row.

Dredging News Online. 2004. "Great Lakes Dredge and Dock." *Dredging News Online,* http://www.sandandgravel.com/news/sponsor/gldd/welcome. html. (July 20, 2004).

Dreyfuss, Robert. 1996. "Tobacco Enemy Number One." *MotherJones,* May/June 1996. http://www.motherjones.com/news/special_reports/ 1996/05/dreyfuss1-2.html. (November 9, 2004).

Dye, Thomas R., and Harmon L. Zeigler. 1996. *The Irony of Democracy: An Uncommon Introduction to American Politics.* Belmont Ca. Harcourt Brace College Publishers.

Educpoint.com. 2004. *Edupoint Educational Systems,* http://www.edupoint.com/ (July 19, 2004).

Eilperin, Juliet. 1996. "Revolving Door Turns Hill's 1994 Departees Into Lobbyists", *Roll Call.* June 3, 1996. http://web.lexis-nexis.com/universe/document?_m=4e6c3ee15f82a074927085e1aa6243 1f&_docnum=1&wchp=dGLbVzz-zSkVA&_md5=5994b155476fb3ab dd130d475ede410e (March 8, 2005).

Eilperin, Juliet. "Ex-Lawmakers' Edge Is Access; Flourishing Class of Lobbyists Capitalizing on Privileges." *Washington Post,* 13 September 2003, A01.

English, Glenn. 2002. *NRECA 2002 Annual Report.* http://www.nreca.org/nreca/ About_Us/About_NRECA/Annual_Report/2002NRECAannual.pdf. (July 28, 2004).

Epstein, Edwin M. 1969. *The Corporation in American Politics.* Englewood Cliffs, NJ: Prentice Hall.

Evans, Richar T. 2003. "The Other Drug War", *Frontline,* Interviewed February 28 2003. http://www.pbs.org/wgbh/pages/frontline/shows/other/ interviews/evans.html. (July 13, 2004).

Federal Election Commission. 1995. *Twenty Year Report.* April http://www.fec.gov/pages/20year.htm. (May 5, 2005).

Federal Election Commission. 1999. http://www.fec.gov/finance/ftpdet.htm. (December 12 1999).

Federal Election Commission. 2001. *FEC Reports on Congressional Financial Activity for 2000: Surpasses $1 Billion Mark.* News Release, Media Advisories May 15, 2001. http://www.fec.gov/press/051501congfinact/ 051501congfinact.html. (January 10 2002).

Federal Election Commission. 2005. *Congressional Campaigns Spend $912 Million Through Late November.* News Release, January 3 2005. http://www.fec.gov/press/press2004/20050103canstat/20050103canstat. html. (February 10, 2005).

Fenno, Richard F., Jr. 1973. *Congressmen in Committees.* Boston: Little, Brown.

Findley, Paul. 1989. *The Dare to Speak Out: People and Institutions Confront Israel's Lobby.* Chicago, Ill: Lawrence Hill Books.

Fiorina Morris P. 1977. *Congress: Keystone to the Washington Establishment.* New Haven: Yale University Press.

Fiorina, Morris P. 1989. *Congress: Keystone of the Washington Establishment.* New Haven, Conn. Yale University Press.

Fiorina, Morris P., David W. Rohde and Peter Wissel. 1975. "Historical Changes in House Turnover." In *Congress in Change. Evolution and Reform,* ed. Norman Ornstein. New York: Praeger.

Food and Drug Administration, et al., Petioners v. Brown and Williamson Tobacco Corporation et al. 2000. 529 U.S. 120.

Fox, Harrison W. and Susan W. Hammons. 1977. *Congressional Staffs: The Invisible force in American Lawmaking.* New York: Free Press.

Frantzich, Stephen E. 1978. "Opting Out: Retirement from the House of Representatives, 1966- 1974." *American Politics Quarterly.* 6:251 -273.

Freeman, J. Leiper. 1965. *The Political Process.* New York: Random House.

Gamson, William. 1968. *Power and Discontent.* Homewood, Il: Dorsey.

Gilligan, Thomas and Keith Krehbiel. 1989. "Asymmetric Information and Legislative Rules with a Heterogeneous Committee." *American Journal of Political Science.* 33:459-90.

Gleick, Elizabeth and Hannah Block. 1996. "Tobacco Blues." *Time,* March 11, 54-59.

Great Lakes Dredge and Dock Corporation. 2000. *Great Lakes Dredge and Dock Corporation: Annual Report Pursuant to Section 13 and 15(d) of the Securities and Exchange Commission Act of 1934,* March 23, 2000. www.sec.gov/Archives/edgar/data/885538/000104746904009789/a213 1439z10-k.htm. (July 21, 2004).

Great Lakes Dredge and Dock Corporation. 2002. *Great Lakes Dredge and Dock Corporation: Annual Report Pursuant to Section 13 and 15(d) of the Securities and Exchange Commission Act of 1934*, March 23, 2000. www.sec.gov/Archives/edgar/data/885538/000110465902000971/j310 2_10k405.htm. (July 21, 2004).

Great Lakes Dredge and Dock Corporation. 2004. *Great Lakes Dredge and Dock Corporation: Annual Report Pursuant to Section 13 and 15(d) of the Securities and Exchange Commission Act of 1934*, March 23, 2000. www.sec.gov/Archives/edgar/data/885538/000104746904009789/a213 1439z10-k.htm. (July 21, 2004).

Great Lakes Dredge and Dock. 2004. "History", *Great Lakes Dredge and Dock.* http://www.gldd.com (July 20, 2004).

Green, Constance McLaughlin. 1962. *Washington: A History of the Capital, 1800-1950.* 1vols. Princeton: Princeton University Press.

Griffith, Ernest S. 1939. *The Impasse of Democracy.* New York: Harrison-Hilton Books.

Groseclose, Timothy and Keith Krehbiel. 1994. "Golden Parachutes, Rubber Checks and Strategic Retirements From the 102d House." *American Journal of Political Science* 38 (February): 75-99.

Grove, Lloyd. 2003. "They're Nervous, but on the Surface They Look Calm and Ready", *Washington Post*, 25 June 2003, C03.

Haider, Donald H. 1974. *When Governments Come To Washington: Governors, Mayors and Intergovernmental Lobbying.* New York: The Free Press.

Hain, Paul L. 1974. "Age, Ambitions, and Political Careers: The Middle Age Crisis." *The Western Political Quarterly* 27 (June): 265-274.

Hall, Richard L. and Robert P. Van Houweling. 1995. "Avarice and Ambition in Congress: Representatives' decisions to run or retire from the U.S. House." *American Political Science Review* 89 (March): 121-135.

Hamilton, Alexander, James Madison, and John Jay. *The Federalist Papers*, Ed. Clinton Rossiter. New York: Penguin Putnam Inc.

Hamilton, Lee H. 2004. "How a Former Member Should View the Congress The Hon. Lee H. Hamilton Luncheon with Association of Former Members" April 22, 2004. http://www.usafmc.org/default. asp?pagenumber=10. (June 29, 2004).

Hamm Keith. 1995. "Patterns of Influence Among Committees, Agencies, and Interest Groups." In *Public Policy Theories, Models and Concepts: An Anthology.* Ed. Daniel C. McCool. Englewood Cliffs NJ: Prentice Hall.

Harbison, Robert. "Lawmakers to Lobbyists: House Democrat Joins March Through Revolving Door," *Christian Science Monitor.* 21 December 1993, A-3.

Hardy, David T. 1986. "The Firearms Owners' Protection Act: A Historical and Legal Perspective." *Cumberland Law Review* 17:585-682. http://www.guncite.com/journals/hardfopa.html#fn*. (November 19, 2004).

Heclo, Hugh. 1995. "Issue Networks and the Executive Establishment." In *Public Policy Theories, Models, and Concepts: An Anthology.* Ed. Daniel C. McCool: Englewood Cliffs, NJ: Prentice Hall.

Heinz, John P., Edward O. Laumann, Robert L. Nelson, and Robert H. Salisbury. 1993. *The Hollow Core: Private Interests in National Policymaking.* Cambridge: Harvard University Press.

Herrick, Rebekah, Michael K Moore, and John R. Hibbing. 1994. "Unfastening the Electoral Connection: The Behavior of U.S. Representatives When Reelection Is No Longer a Factor." *Journal of Politics.* 56 (February): 214-227.

Hibbing, John R. 1982a. "Voluntary Retirements from the House in the Twentieth Century." *The Journal of Politics* 44 (November):1020-1034.

Hibbing, John R. 1982b. *Choosing To Leave: Voluntary Retirement From The U.S. House of Representatives.* Washington DC: University Press of America.

Hibbing, John R. 1986. "Ambition in the House: Behavioral Consequences of Higher Office Goals Among US Representatives." American Journal of Political Science. 30 (August): 651-665.

Hook, Janet. 1992. "Hill's Flock of Lame Ducks: Legislative Wild Cards." *Congressional Quarterly.* (12 September 1992): 2693-2694.

Ik-Whan G. Kwon, Bradley Scott, Scott R. Safranski, and Muen Bae. 1997. "The Effectiveness of gun control laws: Multivariate Statistical Analysis." *The American Journal of Economics and Sociology,* 56 (January): 41-50.

Jacob, Kathryn A. 1995. *Capital Elites: High Society in Washington DC, After the Civil War.* Washington DC: Smithsonian Institute Press.

Jacobson, Gary C. 1992. "Deficit Politics and the 1990 Elections." Presented at the annual meeting of the American Political Science Association, Chicago.

Jakubiak, David. 2004. "Tobacco's Revolving Door To Congress." *Medill News Service.* http://www.medill.northwestern.edu/journalism/mns/washing ton /tobacco/EXCONG.html (June28, 2004).

Jonsson, Patrik. 2004. "Along Tobacco Row, a Changed Culture," *Christian Science Monitor.* 21 October 2004, 1.

Josephy, Alvin M. 1975. *History of the Congress of the United States.* New York: American Heritage Publishing Co.

Kalt, Joseph and Mark Zupan. 1990. "The Apparent Ideological Behavior of Legislatures: Testing for Principal - Agent Slack in Political Institutions." *Journal of Law and Economics.* 33 (April):103-31.

Kernell, Samuel. 1977. "Toward Understanding 19th Century Congressional Careers: Ambition, Competition, and Rotation," *American Journal of Political Science* 21 (November): 669-693.

Kilian, Michael and Arnold Sawislak. 1982. *Who Runs Washington?* New York: St. Martin's Press.

Krehbiel, Keith. 1991. *Information and Legislative Organization.* Ann Arbor: University of Michigan Press.

Labor Force Statistics from the Current Population Survey. 1999. *Union Membership in 1998.* Released January 25 1999. http://stats.bls.gov /newsrels.htm. (March 23, 1999).

Lewis, Charles. 1998. "Statement of Charles Lewis, Chairman and Executive Director," *The Center for Public Integrity,* 9 September 1998, 2.

Lipset, Seymour Martin. 1960. *Political Man.* Garden City, NY: Basic Books.

Lobbying Report for Dawson and Associates. 1999. *Lobbying Report,* http://sopr.senate.gov/cgi-win/opr_gifviewer.exe?/1999/01/ 000/301/00 0301184|3 (July 22, 2004).

Lobbying Report for Dawson and Associates. 2000. *Lobbying Report,* http://sopr.senate.gov/cgi-win/opr_gifviewer.exe?/2000/01/000/343/00 0343658|3 (July 22, 2004).

Lobbying Report for Harold Volkmer. 1998-2002. *Lobbying Report-Mid andYear-end Reprts,* http://sopr.senate.gov/cgi-win/m_opr_viewer.exe?

oFn=3&LOB=VOLKMER,%20HAROLD%20L.&LOBQUAL==
(November 20, 2004).

Lobbying Report for Harold Volkmer. 2002. *Lobbying Report*, http://sopr.senate.gov/cgi-win/opr_gifviewer.exe? (November 20, 2004).

Lobbying Reports for Dickstein, Shapiro Morin and Oshinsky 2004. *Lobbying Reports*, http://sopr.senate.gov/cgi-win/opr_gifviewer.exe?/2004/E/000/05/00005922|4 (November 10, 2004).

Loomis, Burdett A. and Allan J. Cigler. 1991. "Introduction: The Changing Nature of Interest Groups Politics". In *Interest Group Politics* 3rd ed. Allen J. Cigler and Burdett A. Loomis ed. Washington DC: Congressional Quarterly.

Loomis, Burdett. 1984. "On the knife's edge: Public Officials and the Life Cycle", PS: Political Science and Politics 17 (Summer):536-542.

Lott, John R., and Michael Davis. 1992. "A Critical Review and An Extension of the Political Shirking Literature." *Public Choice* 74 (December): 461-84.

Lott, John R., and Robert W. Reed. 1989. "Shirking and Sorting in a Political Market with Finite-lived Politicians." *Public Choice* 61 (April): 75-96.

Lott, John R. 1990. "Attendance Rates, Political Shirking, and the Effect of Post-Elective Office Employment." *Economic Inquiry* 28 (January): 133- 150.

Lowi, Theodore J. 1979. *The End of Liberalism*, 2nd ed. New York: Norton.

Madison, James, Alexander Hamilton, and John Jay 1990. *Federalist Papers.* Ed. George W. Carey and James McClellan. Dubuque IA: Kendall Hunt Publishing Co.

Maraniss, David, and Michael Weisskopf. "Speaker and His Directors Make the Cash Flow Right," *Washington Post*, 27 November 1995, A01.

Marcus, Ruth. "Lobbying's Big Hitters Go to Bat; Some Swat Home Runs, Others Strike Out on Budget Deal," *Washington Post,* 3 August 1997, A01.

Martin, Joseph W. and Robert J. Donovan. 1960. *My First Fifty Years in Politics.* New York: McGraw-Hill.

Mayhew, David R. 1974. *Congress: The Electoral Connection.* New Haven, CT: Yale University Press.

McConnell, Grant. 1966. *Private Power and American Democracy.* New York: Random House.

Michaelis, Laura. 1993. "Annexation Provision is Hurdle Between Two REA Proposals," *Congressional Quarterly Weekly Report* 51(July): 1803.

Milbank, Dana and Glenn Kessler. "Bush Backs China's Stance Reiterates Opposition to Change in Taiwanese Status Quo," *Houston Chronicle,* 10 December 2003, 21A.

Milbrath, Lester W. 1963. *The Washington Lobbyists.* Chicago: Rand McNally and Company.

Miller, Arthur. 1974. "Political Issues and Trust in Government: 1960-1970." *American Political Science Review* 68 (September): 944-61.

Mintz, John. "White House Papers Trace Hughes Executive's Pressure for China Deals," *Washington Post,* 27 July 1998, final edition page A04.

Moore, Michael K. and John R. Hibbing. 1992. "Is Serving in Congress Fun Again? Voluntary Retirements From the House Since the 1970s." *American Journal of Political Science* 36 (August): 824-828.

Moore, Michael K. and John R. Hibbing. 1998. "Situational Dissatisfaction in Congress: Explaining Voluntary Departures." *Journal of Politics* 60 (November): 1088-1107.

Murphy, Kevin. "Lawmakers Find Life After Congress as Lobbyists," *Kansas City Star,* 25 September 1999, A01.

National Education Association. 2002. "Charter Schools," *On the Issues* http://www.nea.org/charter/ (July 17, 2004).

Noah, Timothy. "Why Congressmen Want to be Lobbyists, Part 2." *Slate,* 30 June 2003. http://slate.msn.com/id/2085071/ (June 28, 2004).

Norquist, Grover. 2001. Comments from the 700 Club Show, May 2, 2001.

NRECA. 2002. *NRECA 2002 Annual Report,* http://www.nreca.org/nreca/ About_Us/About_NRECA/Annual_Report/2002NRECAannual.pdf (July 28, 2004).

Parker, Glenn R. 1992. *Institutional Change, Discretion, and the Making of Modern Congress.* Ann Arbor: The University of Michigan Press.

Parker, Glenn R. 1996. *Congress and the Rent-Seeking Society.* Ann Arbor: The University of Michigan Press.

Paxon, Bill. "'If It's Happening on the Hill, Akin Gump is Involved' - Former N.Y. Rep. Bill Paxon Talks Politics from the Other Side of the Lobbying Divide," *The Hill,* 26 March 2003, 15.

Petracca, Mark P. 1992. "The Rediscovery of Interest Group Politics," in *The Politics of Interests: Interest Groups Transformed.* Mark Petracca ed. Boulder, CO: Westview Press.

Pincus, Walter and John Mintz. "Report Faults Hughes on Data Given China," *Washington Post,* 9 December 1998, A22.

Pitkin, Hanna F. 1967. *The Concept of Representation.* Berkeley: University of California Press.

Polsby, Nelson W. 1968. "The Institutionalization of the House of Representatives." *American Political Science Review* 62(1): 146-147.

Poole, Claire. 1998. "School's In," *Texas Monthly,* September 3, 24.

Powell, Marjorie. 2003. "The Other Drug War," *Frontline,* Interviewed February 14. http://www.pbs.org/wgbh/pages/frontline/ shows/other/ (July 13, 2004).

Prewitt, K. 1969. *The Recruitment of Political Leaders: A Study of Citizen Politicians.* Indianapolis: Bobbs-Merrill.

Prewitt, Kenneth and William Nowlin. 1969. "Political Ambitions and the Behavior of Incumbent Politicians." *The Western Political Quarterly* 22 (June): 298-308.

Price, Douglas H. 1975. "Congress and the Evolution of Legislative 'Professionalism', in *Congress in Change*, ed. Norman J. Ornstein. New York: Praeger.

Public Law 103-129.1993. Rural Electrification Loan Restructuring Act of 1993.

Remer, David R. "Ex-Lawmakers' Edge is Access," *Washington Post,* 13 September 2003, A01.

Riggs, Frank. 1997a. *Hearings before the Subcommittee on Early Childhood, Youth and Families of the Committee on Education and the Workforce House of Representatives: One Hundred Fifth Congress, first session.* Serial Number 105-13. Government Printing Office, Washington DC.

Riggs, Frank. 1997b. "Opening Remarks: The Honorable Frank Riggs (R-CA) *Markup of H.R. 2616, Charter Schools Amendments Act of 1997*, October 9, http://edworkforce.house.gov/markups/105th/fc/hr2616 /109sr.htm (July 20, 2004).

Rohde, David W. 1979. "Risk-Bearing and Progressive Ambition: The Case of Members of the United States House of Representatives." *American Journal of Political Science* 23 (February): 1 -26.

Rohde, David W. 1991. *Parties And Leaders in the Postreform House.* Chicago: University of Chicago Press.

Rothstein, Richard. 1998. "Charter Conundrum," *The American Prospect*, 39 (July-August): 46-60.

Russell Chaddock, Gail. 2003. "Republicans Take Over K Street," *The Christian Science Monitor.* 29 August. http://www.csmonitor.com/2003/0829 /p01s01-uspo.html (July 1, 2004).

Sack, Joetta, L., and Anjetta McQueen. 1998. "Federal Files." *Education Week,* December 16: 23.

Sandburg, Carl.1926. *Abraham Lincoln: The Prairie Years.* Vol. 1. New York: Harcourt Brace and Co.

Schlesinger, Joseph. 1966. *Ambition and Politics: Political Careers in the United States.* Chicago: Rand McNally.

Schlozman, Kay Lehman and John T. Tierney. 1986. *Organized Interests and American Democracy.* New York: Harper and Row.

Schwartz, Robert. 1994. "Restructuring Philadelphia's Neighborhood High Schools: A Conversation with Constance Clayton and Michelle Fine," *The Journal of Negro Education* 63 (Winter): 111-125.

Shaiko, Ronald G. 1998. "Lobbying in Washington: A Contemporary Perspective". In *The Interest Group Connection: Electioneering, Lobbying, and Policymaking in Washington.* ed. Paul S. Herrnson, Ronald G. Shaiko and Clyde Wilcox. Chatham, NJ: Chatham House Publishers, Inc.

Shepsle, Kenneth A and Barry R. Weingast. 1987. "The Institutional Foundations of Committee Power," *American Political Science Review* 81(March): 85-104.

Shepsle, Kenneth A. 1979. "Institutional Arrangements and Equilibrium in Multidimensional Voting Models," *American Journal of Political Science* 23 (February): 27-59.

Shuldiner, Allan and CRP Staff. 1999. "Influence, Inc. The Bottom Line on Washington Lobbying," 1999 edition. *Center for Responsive Politics. http://www.opensecrets.org/lobbyists/index.htm. As of 1-12-00.*

The Committee on Standards of Official Conduct. 1992. *Ethics Manual for Members, Officers, and Employees of the U.S. House of Representatives*. U.S. Government Printing Office 53-077 Washington: 1992, http://www.house.gov/Ethics/Ethicforward.html (July 2004).

Theriault, Sean M. 1998. "Moving Up or Moving Out: Career Ceilings and Congressional Retirement," *Legislative Studies Quarterly* 23 (August): 419- 433.

Tocqueville, Alexis de. 1960. *Democracy in America*. New York: Vintage.

Truman, David. 1971. *The Governmental Process* 2nd ed. New York: Knopf.

U.S. Government Printing Office. 1999. *Historical Tables: Budget of the United States Government Fiscal Year 2000.* Washington D.C.

United States General Accounting Office. National Security and International Affairs Division. 2000. *Report to the Chairman and Ranking Minority Member, Subcommittee on Readiness, and Management Support, Committee on Armed Services, US Senate: Defense Trade Contractors Engage in Varied International Alliances*. Washington: United States General Accounting Office.

United States House of Representatives. 1998. *House Rpt.105-582 – To Establish The Select Committee On U.S. National Security And Military/Commercial Concerns With The People's Republic Of China*, June 16. http://frwebgate.access.gpo.gov/cgi-bin/getdoc.cgi?dbname= 105_cong_reports&docid=f:hr582.105.pdf (November 26, 2004).

United States Senate Office of Public Records. 2004. http://sopr.senate.gov/ (July 19, 2004).

US Charter Schools. 2004. "History," *US Charter Schools*. http://www. uscharterschools.org/pub/uscs_docs/o/history.htm (July 17, 2004).

US Department of Education. 2000. "The State of Charter Schools 2000: Fourth Year Report," January 2000, http://www.ed.gov/pubs/charter4thyear/ index.html (July 17, 2004).

US Department of State Office of the Spokesman. 2003. "US Department of State Reaches Settlement with Boeing and Hughes," March 5, 2003. Washington DC. http://www.state.gov/r/pa/prs/ps/2003/18275.htm (December 7, 2004).

Vandehei, Jim and Kathleen Day. "Oxley May Face Ethics Probe: Key House Chairman Under Fire for Pressuring Lobby Group," *Washington Post*, 26 February 2003, A04.

158

Walker, Charls. 1998. "A Four-Decade Perspective on Lobbying in Washington," in *The Interest Group Connection: Electioneering, Lobbying, and Policymaking in Washington.* ed. Paul S. Herrnson, Ronald G. Shaiko and Clyde Wilcox. Chatham, NJ: Chatham House Publishers, Inc.

Walker, Jack L. 1983. "The Origins and Maintenance of Interest Groups in America," *American Political Science Review.* 77 (June): 390-406.

Warren, Charles. 1928. *The Making of the Constitution.* Boston: Little, Brown.

Weatherford, M. Stepen. 1992. "Measuring Political Legitimacy." *American Political Science Review* 86 (March):149-166.

Whitehurst, William G. 2001. "Lobbies and Political Action Comittees: A Congressman's Perspective", *Inside the House: Former Members Reveal How Congress Really Works*, ed. Lou Frey Jr. and Michael T. Hayes. Lanham, MD: University Press of America.

Young, James Sterling. 1966. *The Washington Community: 1800-1828.* New York: Columbia University Press.

About the Author

Dr. Adolfo Santos is a professor of political science at the University of Houston-Downtown, where he has been teaching since 1997. He received his doctoral degree from the University of Houston in 1998. Dr. Santos specializes on the US Congress and minority representation.

Index